The World's Best Short Stories

Anthology & Criticism

Volume X

Research & Reference

THE WORLD'S BEST SERIES

The World's Best Short Stories

I.	*Short Story Masters: Early 19th Century*
II.	*Short Story Masters: Late 19th & Early 20th Centuries*
III.	*Famous Stories*
IV.	*Fables and Tales*
V.	*Mystery and Detection*
VI.	*Horror and Science Fiction*
VII.	*Characters*
VIII.	*Places*
IX.	*Cultures*
X.	*Research & Reference*

The World's Best Poetry

Foundation Volumes I - X

Supplements:

I.	*20th Century English & American Verse, 1900-1929*
II.	*20th Century English & American Verse, 1930-1950*
III.	*Critical Companion*
IV.	*Minority Poetry of America*
V.	*20th Century Women Poets*
VI.	*20th Century African & Latin American Verse*
VII.	*20th Century Asian Verse*
VIII.	*Cumulative Index*

CoreFiche: The World's Best Drama
Microfiche with companion reference

The World's Best Short Stories

Anthology & Criticism

Volume X

Research & Reference

Essays by Allen, Brandes, Brownell, Cooper, Howells, James, Mabie, Matthews, Peck, Phelps, Poe, Sherman, Twain

Prepared by
The Editorial Board

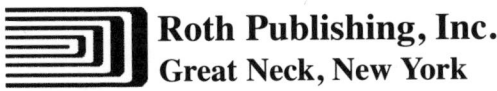
Roth Publishing, Inc.
Great Neck, New York

Copyright © 1996 Roth Publishing, Inc.
All rights reserved.

ISBN 0-89609-316-6
ISBN for 10 Volume Set 0-89609-400-6
Library of Congress Catalog Card Number 89-60440

Manufactured in the U.S.A.

Contents

Preface vii

Introduction ix

The Art of Fiction 1
   Henry James

Critical Remarks on Hawthorne's *Twice-Told Tales* 25
   Edgar Allan Poe

On Poe 35
   William Crary Brownell

The Detective Story 67
   Harry Thurston Peck

On O. Henry 83
   Frederic Taber Cooper

On Ambrose Bierce 97
   Frederic Taber Cooper

The Deterioration of the Short Story 111
   James Lane Allen

The Washington Irving Country 117
   Hamilton Wright Mabie

The Utopian Naturalism of H. G. Wells 131
   Stuart Pratt Sherman

On Mark Twain 143
   Brander Matthews

On Gogol 161
   William Lyon Phelps

On Balzac 179
   George Brandes

On William Dean Howells 201
   Mark Twain

Some Anomalies of the Short Story 211
   William Dean Howells

Preface

The World's Best Short Stories is designed to give both the serious student and the general reader a large selection and broad range of stories from around the world. Its ten volumes organize the stories into reader-friendly groupings:

Short Story Masters (Volumes I and II)
Famous Stories (Volume III)
Fables and Tales (Volume IV)
Mystery and Detection (Volume V)
Horror and Science Fiction (Volume VI)
Characters (Volume VII)
Places (Volume VIII)
Cultures (Volume IX)
Research & Reference (Volume X)

The arrangement of the stories suggests the multiple approaches for using these volumes. *Short Story Masters* focuses on the author; it contains stories that demonstrate the development of the short story as a conscious art form. *Famous Stories* is the volume to go to for well-known stories by authors who may or may not themselves be well-known. *Fables and Tales* includes fairy tales and other short non-realistic literature, as well as tales that are ancestors of the short story form. Volumes V and VI contain genre fiction; they act as a kind of counterpart to *Short Story Masters*. Whereas *Masters* places the short story in the tradition of an evolving art, these genre-centered volumes put it at the disposal of the general reader and the popular imagination. *Mystery and Detection* makes the case for a genre that has been continuously popular and critically treated since Poe, while *Horror and Science Fiction* looks at two different styles of fantastic literature—one finding its elements in the supernatural, the other in the superscientific.

The later volumes contain stories that are remarkable for a salient feature. The stories in *Characters* are portrait studies: their primary function is to examine the character of the hero or heroine. *Places* compiles stories that evoke a setting in a way that is memorable and important to the being of the story. *Cultures* uses ethnicity as its backdrop. It includes stories that are informed by their cultural setting. Finally, Volume X is a research and reference volume, containing essays by and on many of the authors whose works are included in the earlier volumes.

The organization, variety, and breadth of **The World's Best Short Stories** makes it a unique anthology collection that can be used for study or read for pleasure.

Introduction

The World's Best Short Stories collection concludes it's ten-volume set with this volume, *Research & Reference*, a collection of essays both by and about many of the authors whose stories appear in the earlier volumes. Edgar Allan Poe's important review of Nathaniel Hawthorne's *Twice-Told Tales*, American literature's first elucidation of an aesthetic theory of the short story, is here, as is William Dean Howells' attempt to explain the poor showing by collections of short stories in the publishing marketplace, "Some Anomalies of the Short Story." The selected essays are often thematically interrelated, presenting diverging points of view on similar issues. After Poe's review of Hawthorne's tales, for example, you'll find an essay about Poe and his work by W. C. Brownell, who is sharply critical of Poe's execution of his own theories, and the text of an interview with James Lane Allen, who offers yet another opinion on the short story's debt to Poe and some ideas on the general state of short fiction in the post-Civil War era. Similarly, William Lyon Phelps' essay on Gogol, the progenitor of Russian realistic fiction, may spur an interest in critical treatments of other realist writers, which may be further satisfied by George Brandes' piece on Balzac, or Mark Twain's comments on William Dean Howells.

As a collection, this volume provides a coherent framework for the study and appreciation of some of the major figures and works included in volumes I through IX. Introductions describing important points and noting particular significances precede each essay. See Volume IX for a cumulative index to all authors and stories in the complete **World's Best Short Stories** set.

The Art of Fiction

Henry James

One of the most renowned tracts on literary art in the English language, Henry James' essay on fiction is brimming with his theories on and considerations of the two arts of literary composition and criticism. What are the rules that should govern the fiction writer's process? Where should one begin in judging the merits and short-comings of a particular piece of writing? James, responding throughout the essay to another essay on a similar theme by the 19th-century novelist and critic Walter Besant, presents his answers to these and other important questions surrounding fiction in general. Particularly notable for what might be most accurately called it's "tolerance," the essay attacks those literary guidelines, proffered by Besant and his contemporaries, that would limit the scope of fiction to certain topics, limit the reach of an author to that experience which is his or hers only in the most superficial sense of the word, and reject all purposes in fiction writing and reading save instruction and amusement. This is not to say that James is without his own biases. He, for example, asserts that "the only reason for the existence of a novel is that it does attempt to represent life." Since this essay's composition, much 20th-century criticism has cast doubt upon fiction's ability to represent existence and the ability of any writer to create an objective portrait of reality that is not biased by his or her own ideologies, literary and otherwise. Today's literary theorists would have as much to quibble with in James' essay as he found in Besant's. They would, however, agree upon James' modest assertion that "the successful application of any art is a delightful spectacle, but the theory too is interesting." But the value of "The Art of Fiction" resides not necessarily in the timeless literary truths it contains (for many of James' stances have survived a century's worth of fictional practice and criticism, while others have fallen at the hands of new schools and movements), but rather in it's function as a literary-historical document that both describes the intellectual climate of one of the most productive periods in American and English fiction, and records the theories of one of world literature's most imposing and enduring figures.

I should not have fixed so comprehensive a title to these few remarks, necessarily wanting in any completeness upon a subject the full consideration of which would carry us far, did I not seem to discover a pretext for my temerity in the interesting pamphlet lately published under this name by Walter Besant. Besant's lecture at the Royal Institution—the original form of his pamphlet—appears to indicate that many persons are interested in the art of fiction, and are not indifferent to such remarks as those who practice it may attempt to make about it. I am therefore anxious not to lose the benefit of this favorable association, and to edge in a few words under cover of the attention which Besant is sure to have excited. There is something very encouraging in his having put into form certain of his ideas on the mystery of story-telling.

It is a proof of life and curiosity—curiosity on the part of the brotherhood of novelists as well as on the part of their readers. Only a short time ago it might have been supposed that the English novel was not what the French call *discutable.* It had no air of having a theory, a conviction, a consciousness of itself behind it—of being the expression of an artistic faith, the result of choice and comparison. I do not say it was necessarily the worse for that: it would take much more courage than I possess to intimate that the form of novel as Dickens and Thackeray (for instance) saw it had any taint of incompleteness. It was, however, *naif* (if I may help myself out with another French word); and evidently if it be destined to suffer in any way for having lost its naivete it has now an idea of making sure of the corresponding advantages. During the period I have alluded to there was a comfortable good-humored feeling abroad that a novel is a novel, as a pudding is a pudding, and that our only business with it could be to swallow it. But within a year or two, for some reason or other, there have been signs of returning animation—the era of discussion would appear to have been to a certain extent opened. Art lives upon discussion, upon experiment, upon curiosity, upon variety of attempt, upon the exchange of views and the comparison of standpoints; and there is a presumption that those times when no one has anything particular to say about it, and has no reason to give for practice or preference, though they may be times of honor, are not times of development—are times, possibly, even a little of dullness. The successful application of any art is a delightful spectacle, but the theory too is interesting; and though there is a great deal of the latter without the former I suspect there has never been a genuine success that has not had a latent core of conviction. Discussion, suggestion, formulation, these things are fertilizing when they are frank and sincere. Besant has set an excellent example in saying what he thinks, for his part, about the way in which fiction should be written, as well as about the way in which it should be published; for his view of the "art," carried on into an appendix, covers that too. Other laborers in the same field will doubtless take up the argument, they will give it the light of their experience, and the effect will surely be to make our interest in the novel a little more what it had for some time threatened to fail to be—

a serious, active, inquiring interest, under protection of which this delightful study may, in moments of confidence, venture to say a little more what it thinks of itself.

It must take itself seriously for the public to take it so. The old superstition about fiction being "wicked" has doubtless died out in England; but the spirit of it lingers in a certain oblique regard directed toward any story which does not more or less admit that it is only a joke. Even the most jocular novel feels in some degree the weight of the proscription that was formerly directed against literary levity: the jocularity does not always succeed in passing for orthodoxy. It is still expected, though perhaps people are ashamed to say it, that a production which is after all only a "make-believe" (for what else is a "story?") shall be in some degree apologetic— shall renounce the pretension of attempting really to represent life. This, of course, any sensible, wide-awake story declines to do, for it quickly perceives that the tolerance granted to it on such a condition is only an attempt to stifle it disguised in the form of generosity. The old evangelical hostility to the novel, which was as explicit as it was narrow, and which regarded it as little less favorable to our immortal part than a stage-play, was in reality far less insulting. The only reason for the existence of a novel is that it does attempt to represent life. When it relinquishes this attempt, the same attempt that we see on the canvas of the painter, it will have arrived at a very strange pass. It is not expected of the picture that it will make itself humble in order to be forgiven; and the analogy between the art of the painter and the art of the novelist is, so far as I am able to see, complete. Their inspiration is the same, their process (allowing for the different quality of the vehicle) is the same, their success is the same. They may learn from each other, they may explain and sustain each other. Their cause is the same, and the honor of one is the honor of another. The Mahometans think a picture an unholy thing, but it is a long time since any Christian did, and it is therefore the more odd that in the Christian mind the traces (dissimulated though they may be) of a suspicion of the sister art should linger to this day. The only effectual way to lay it to rest is to emphasize the analogy to which I just alluded—to insist on the fact that as the picture is reality, so the novel is history. That is the only general description (which does it justice) that we may give of the novel. But history also is allowed to represent life; it is not, any more than painting, expected to apologize. The subject-matter of fiction is stored up likewise in documents and records, and if it will not give itself away, as they say in California, it must speak with assurance, with the tone of the historian. Certain accomplished novelists have a habit of giving themselves away which must often bring tears to the eyes of people who take their fiction seriously. I was lately struck, in reading over many pages of Anthony Trollope, with his want of discretion in this regard. In a digression, a parenthesis or an aside, he concedes to the reader that he and this trusting friend are only "making believe." He admits that the events he narrates have not really happened, and that he can give his narrative any turn the reader may like best. Such a betrayal of a sacred office seems to me, I confess, a terrible crime; it is what I mean by the attitude of apology, and it shocks me every whit as much in Trollope as it would have shocked me in Gibbon or Macaulay. It implies that the novelist is less occupied in looking for the truth (the truth, of course I mean, that he assumes, the premises that we must grant him, whatever they may be) than the historian, and in doing so it deprives him at a stroke of all his standing-room. To represent and illustrate the past, the actions of man, is the task of either writer, and the only difference that I can see is, in proportion as he succeeds, to the honor of the novelist, consisting as it does in his having more difficulty in collecting his evidence, which is so far from being purely literary. It seems to me to give him a great character, the fact that he has at once so much in common with the philosopher and the painter; this double analogy is a magnificent heritage.

It is of all this evidently that Besant is full when he insists upon the fact that fiction is one of the fine arts, deserving in its turn of all the honors and emoluments that have hitherto been reserved for the successful professions of music, poetry, painting, architecture. It is impossible to insist too much on so important a truth, and the place that Besant demands for the work of the novelist may be represented, a trifle less abstractly, by saying that he demands not only that it shall be reputed artistic, but that it shall be reputed very artistic indeed. It is excellent that he should have struck this note, for his doing so indicates that there was need of it, that his proposition may be to many people a novelty. One rubs one's eyes at the thought; but the rest of Besant's essay confirms the revelation. I suspect in truth that it would be possible to confirm it still further, and that one would not be far wrong in saying that in addition to the people to whom it has never occurred that a novel ought to be artistic, there are a great many others who, if this principle were urged upon them, would be filled with an indefinable mistrust. They would find it difficult to explain their repugnance, but it would operate strongly to put them on their guard. "Art," in our Protestant communities, where so many things have got so strangely twisted about, is supposed in certain circles to have some vague injurious effect upon those who make it an important consideration, who let it weigh in the balance. It is assumed to be opposed in some mysterious manner to morality, to amusement, to instruction. When it is embodied in the work of the painter (the sculptor is another affair!) you know what it is: it stands there before you, the honesty of pink and green and a gilt frame; you can see the worst of it at a glance, and you can be on your guard. But when it is introduced into literature it becomes more insidious—there is danger of its hurting you before you know it. Literature should be either instructive or amusing, and there is in many minds an impression that these artistic preoccupations, the search of form, contribute to neither end, interfere indeed with both. They are too frivolous to be edifying, and too serious to be diverting; and they are moreover priggish and paradoxical and superfluous. That, I think, represents the manner in which the latent thought of many people who read novels as an exercise in skipping would explain itself if it were to become articulate. They would argue, of course, that a novel ought to be "good," but they would interpret this term in a fashion of their own, which indeed would vary considerably from one critic to another. One would say that being good means representing virtuous and aspiring characters placed in prominent positions; another would say that it depends on a "happy ending," on a distribution at the last of prizes, pensions, husbands, wives, babies, millions, appended paragraphs, and cheerful remarks. Another still would say that it means being full of incident and movement, so that we shall wish to jump ahead, to see who was the mysterious stranger, and if the stolen will was ever found, and shall not be distracted from this pleasure by any tiresome analysis or "description." But they would all agree that the "artistic" idea would spoil some of their fun. One would hold it accountable for all the description, another would see it revealed in the absence of sympathy. Its hostility to a happy ending would be evident, and it might even in some cases render any ending at all impossible. The "ending" of a novel is, for many persons, like that of a good dinner, a course of dessert and ices, and the artist in fiction is regarded as a sort of meddlesome doctor who forbids agreeable aftertastes. It is therefore true that this conception of Besant's of the novel as a superior form encounters not only a negative but a positive indifference. It matters little that as a work of art it should really be as little or as much of its essence to supply happy endings, sympathetic characters, and an objective tone, as if it were a work of mechanics: the association of ideas, however incongruous, might easily be too much for it if an eloquent voice were not sometimes raised to call attention to the fact that it is at once as free and as serious a branch of literature as any other.

Certainly this might sometimes be doubted in presence of the enormous number of works of fiction that appeal to the credulity of our generation for it might easily seem that there could be no great character in a commodity so quickly and easily produced. It must be admitted that good novels are much compromised by bad ones, and that the field at large suffers discredit from overcrowding. I think, however, that this injury is only superficial, and that the superabundance of written fiction proves nothing against the principle itself. It has been vulgarized, like all other kinds of literature, like everything else today, and it has proved, more than some kinds, accessible to vulgarization. But there is as much difference as there ever was between a good novel and a bad one: the bad is swept with all the daubed canvases and spoiled marble into some unvisited limbo, or infinite rubbish-yard beneath the back-windows of the world, and the good subsists and emits its light and stimulates our desire for perfection. As I shall take the liberty of making but a single criticism of Besant, whose tone is so full of love of his art, I may as well have done with it at once. He seems to me to mistake, in attempting to say so definitely beforehand, what sort of an affair the good novel will be. To indicate the danger of such an error as that has been the purpose of these few pages; to suggest that certain traditions on the subject, applied *a priori*, have already had much to answer for, and that the good health of an art which undertakes so immediately to reproduce life must demand that it be perfectly free. It lives upon exercise, and the very meaning of exercise is freedom. The only obligation to which in advance we may hold a novel, without incurring the accusation of being arbitrary, is that it be interesting. That general responsibility rests upon it, but it is the only one I can think of. The ways in which it is at liberty to accomplish this result (of interesting us) strike me as innumerable, and such as can only suffer from being marked out or fenced in my prescription. They are as various as the temperament of man, and they are successful in proportion as they reveal a particular mind, different from others. A novel is in its broadest definition a personal, a direct impression of life: that, to begin with, constitutes its value, which is greater or less according to the intensity of the impression. But there will be no intensity at all, and therefore no value, unless there is freedom to feel and say. The tracing of a line to be followed, of a tone to be taken, of a form to be filled out, is a limitation of that freedom and a suppression of the very thing that we are most curious about. The form, it seems to me, is to be appreciated after the fact: then the author's choice has been made, his standard has been indicated; then we can follow lines and directions and compare tones and resemblances. Then in a word we can enjoy one of the most charming of pleasures, we can estimate quality, we can apply the test of execution. The execution belongs to the author alone; it is what is most personal to him, and we measure him by that. The advantage, the luxury, as well as the torment and responsibility of the novelist, is that there is no limit to what he may attempt as an executant—no limit to his possible experiments, efforts, discoveries, successes. Here it is especially that he works, step by step, like his brother of the brush, of whom we may always say that he has painted his picture in a manner best known to himself. His manner is his secret, not necessarily a jealous one. He cannot disclose it as a general thing if he would; he would be at a loss to teach it to others. I say this with a due recollection of having insisted on the community of method of the artist who writes a novel. The painter is able to teach the rudiments of his practice, and it is possible, from the study of good work (granted the aptitude), both to learn how to paint and to learn how to write. Yet it remains true, without injury to the rapprochement, that the literary artist would be obliged to say to his pupil much more than the other, "Ah, well, you must do it as you can!" It is a question of degree, a matter of delicacy. If there are exact sciences, there are also exact arts, and the grammar of painting is so much more definite that it makes the difference.

I ought to add, however, that if Besant says at the beginning of his essay that the "laws of fiction may be laid down and taught with as much precision and exactness as the laws of harmony, perspective, and proportion," he mitigates what might appear to be an extravagance by applying his remark to "general" laws, and by expressing most of these rules in a manner with which it would certainly be unaccomodating to disagree. That the novelist must write from his experience, that his "characters must be real and such as might be met with in actual life," that "a young lady brought up in a quiet country village should avoid descriptions of garrison life," and "a writer whose friends and personal experiences belong to the lower middle-class should carefully avoid introducing his characters into society," that one should enter one's notes in a common-place book, that one's figures should be clear in outline, that making them clear by some trick of speech or of carriage is a bad method, and "describing them at length" is a worse one, that English fiction should have a "conscious moral purpose," that "it is almost impossible to estimate too highly the value of careful workmanship—that is, of style," that "the most important point of all is the story," that "the story is everything"— these are principles with most of which it is surely impossible not to sympathize. That remark about the lower middle-class writer and his knowing his place is perhaps rather chilling; but for the rest I should find it difficult to dissent from any one of these recommendations. At the same time, I should find it difficult positively to assent to them, with the exception, perhaps, of the injunction as to entering one's notes in a commonplace book. They scarcely seem to me to have the quality that Besant attributes to the rules of the novelist—the "precision and exactness" of "the laws of harmony, perspective, and proportion." They are suggestive, they are even inspiring, but they are not exact, though they are doubtless as much so as the case admits of, which is a proof of the liberty of interpretation for which I just contended. For the value of these different injunctions—so beautiful and so vague—is wholly in the meaning one attaches to them. The characters, the situation, which strike one as real will be those that touch and interest one most, but the measure of reality is very difficult to fix. The reality of Don Quixote or of Micawber is a very delicate shade; it is a reality so colored by the author's vision that, vivid as it may be, one would hesitate to propose it as a model: one would expose one's self to some very embarrassing questions on the part of a pupil. It goes without saying that you will not write a good novel unless you possess the sense of reality; but it will be difficult to give you a recipe for calling that sense into being. Humanity is immense, and reality has a myriad forms; the most one can affirm is that some of the flowers of fiction have the odor of it, and others have not; as for telling you in advance how your nosegay should be composed, that is another affair. It is equally excellent and inconclusive to say that one must write from experience; to our supposing aspirant such a declaration might savor of mockery. What kind of experience is intended, and where does it begin and end? Experience is never limited, and it is never complete; it is an immense sensibility, a kind of huge spider web of the finest silken threads suspended in the chamber of consciousness, and catching every air-borne particle in its tissue. It is the very atmosphere of the mind; and when the mind is imaginative—much more when it happens to be that of a person of genius—it takes to itself the faintest hints of life, it converts the very pulses of the air into revelations. The young lady living in a village has only to be a damsel upon whom nothing is lost to make it quite unfair (as it seems to me) to declare to her that she shall have nothing to say about the military. Greater miracles have been seen than that, imagination assisting, she should speak the truth about some of these gentlemen. I remember an English novelist, a woman of genius, telling me that she was much commended for the impression she had managed to give in one of her tales of the nature and way of life of the French Protestant youth. She had been asked where she learned so much about this recondite being, she had been congratulated on her peculiar opportunities. These opportunities consisted in her having once, in Paris, as she descended a staircase, passed an open door where, in the household of a *pasteur*, some of the young Protestants were seated at table round a finished meal. The glimpse made a picture; it lasted only a moment, but that moment was experience. She had gotten her direct personal impression, and she turned out her type. She knew what youth was, and what Protestantism; she also had the advantage of having seen what it was to be French, so that she converted these ideas into a concrete image and produced a reality. Above all, however, she was blessed with the faculty which when you give it an inch takes a mile, and which for the artist is a much greater source of strength than any accident of residence or of place in the social scale. The power to guess the unseen from the seen, to trace the implication of things, to judge the whole piece by the pattern, the condition of feeling life in general so completely that you are well on your way to knowing any particular corner of it—this cluster of gifts may almost be said to constitute experience, and they occur in country and in town, and in the most differing stages of education. If experience consists of impressions, it may be said that impressions are experience, just as (have we not seen it?) they are the very air we breathe. Therefore, if I should certainly say to a novice, "Write from experience and from experience only," I should feel that this was rather a tantalizing monition if I were not careful immediately to add, "Try to be one of the people on whom nothing is lost!"

I am far from intending by this to minimize the importance of exactness—of truth of detail. One can speak best from one's own taste, and I may therefore venture to say that the air of reality (solidity of specification) seems to me to be the supreme virtue of a novel—the merit on which all its other merits (including that conscious moral purpose of which Besant speaks) helplessly and submissively depend. If it be not there they are all as nothing, and if these be there, they owe their effect to the success with which the author has produced the illusion of life. The cultivation of this success, the study of this exquisite process, form, to my taste, the beginning and the end of the art of the novelist. They are his inspiration, his despair, his reward, his torment, his delight. It is here in very truth that he competes with life; it is here that he competes with his brother the painter in his attempt to render the look of things, the look that conveys their meaning, to catch the color, the relief, the expression, the surface, the substance of the human spectacle. It is in regard to this that Besant is well inspired when he bids him take notes. He cannot possibly take too many, he cannot possibly take enough. All life solicits him, and to "render" the simplest surface, to produce the most momentary illusion, is a very complicated business. His case would be easier, and the rule would be more exact, if Besant had been able to tell him what notes to take. But this, I fear, he can never learn in any manual; it is the business of his life. He has to take a great many in order to select a few, he has to work them up as he can, and even the guides and philosophers who might have most to say to him must leave him alone when it comes to the application of precepts, as we leave the painter in communion with his palette. That his characters "must be clear in outline," as Besant says—he feels that down to his boots; but how he shall make them so is a secret between his good angel and himself. It would be absurdly simple if he could be taught that a great deal of "description" would make them so, or that on the contrary the absence of description and the cultivation of dialogue, or the absence of dialogue and the multiplication of "incident," would rescue him from his difficulties. Nothing, for instance, is more possible than that he be of a turn of mind for which this odd, literal opposition of description and dialogue, incident and description, has little meaning and light. People often talk of these things as if they had a kind of internecine distinctness, instead of melting into each other at every breath, and being intimately associated parts of one general effort of expression. I cannot imagine composition existing in a series of blocks, nor conceive, in any novel worth discussing at all, of a passage of description that is not in its intention narrative, a passage of dialogue that is not in its intention descriptive, a touch of truth of any sort that does not partake of the nature of incident, or an incident that derives its interest from any other source than the general and only source of the success of a work of art—that of being illustrative. A novel is a living thing, all one and continuous, like any other organism, and in proportion as it lives will it be found, I think, that in each of the parts there is something of each of the other parts. The critic who over the close texture of a finished work shall pretend to trace a geography of items will mark some frontiers as artificial, I fear, as any that have been known to history. There is an old-fashioned distinction between the novel of character and the novel of incident which must have cost many a smile to the intending fabulist who was keen about his work. It appears to me as little to the point as the equally celebrated distinction between the novel and the romance—to answer as little to any reality. There are bad novels and good novels, as there are bad pictures and good pictures; but that is the only distinction in which I see any meaning, and I can as little imagine speaking of a novel of character as I can imagine speaking of a picture of character. When one says picture one says of character, when one says novel one says of incident, and the terms may be transposed at will. What is character but the determination of incident? What is incident but the illustration of character? What is either a picture or a novel that is not of character? What else do we seek in it and find in it? It is an incident for a woman to stand up with her hand resting on a table and look at you in a certain way; or if it be not an incident I think it will be hard to say what it is. At the same time it is an expression of character. If you say you don't see it (character in that—*allons donc!*), this is exactly what the artist who has reasons of his own for thinking he does see it undertakes to show you. When a young man makes up his mind that he has not faith enough after all to enter the church as he intended, that is an incident, though you may not hurry to the end of the chapter to see whether perhaps he doesn't change once more. I do not say that these are extraordinary or startling incidents. I do not pretend to estimate the degree of interest proceeding from them, for this will depend upon the skill of the painter. It sounds almost puerile to say that some incidents are intrinsically much more important than others, and I need not take this precaution after having professed my sympathy for the major ones in remarking that the only classification of the novel that I can understand is into that which has life and that which has it not.

The novel and the romance, the novel of incident and that of character—these clumsy separations appear to me to have been made by critics and readers for their own convenience, and to help them out of some of their occasional predicaments, but to have little reality or interest for the producer, from whose point of view it is of course that we are attempting to consider the art of fiction. The case is the same with another shadowy category which Besant apparently is disposed to set up—that of the "modern English novel," unless indeed it be that in this matter he has fallen into an accidental confusion of standpoints. It is not quite clear whether he intends the remarks in which he alludes to it to be didactic or historical. It is as difficult to suppose a person intending to write a modern English as to suppose him writing an ancient English novel: that is a label which begs the question. One writes the novel, one paints the picture of one's language and of one's time, and calling it modern English will not, alas, make the difficult task any easier. No more, unfortunately, will calling this or that work of one's fellow-artist a romance—unless it be, of course, simply for the pleasantness of the thing, as for instance when Hawthorne gave this heading to his story of Blithedale. The French, who have brought the theory of fiction to remarkable completeness, have but one name for the novel, and have not attempted smaller things in it, that I can see, for that. I can think of no obligation to which the "romancer" would not be held equally with the novelist; the standard of execution is equally high for each. Of course it is of execution that we are talking—that being the only point of a novel that is open to contention. This perhaps too often lost sight of, only to produce interminable confusions and cross-purposes. We must grant the artist his subject, his idea, his *donnee*: our criticism is applied only to what he makes of it. Naturally I do not mean that we are bound to like it or find it interesting: in case we do not our course is perfectly simple—to let it alone. We may believe that of a certain idea even the most sincere novelist can make nothing at all, and the event may perfectly justify our belief; but the failure will have been a failure to execute, and it is in the execution that the fatal weakness is recorded. If we pretend to respect the artist at all, we must allow him his freedom of choice, in the face, in particular cases, of innumerable presumptions that the choice will not fructify. Art derives a considerable part of its beneficial exercise from flying in the face of presumptions and some of the most interesting experiments of which it is capable are hidden in the bosom of common things. Gustave Flaubert has written a story about the devotion of a servant girl to a parrot, and the production, highly finished as it is, cannot on the whole be called a success. We are perfectly free to find it flat, but I think it might have been interesting; and I, for my part, am extremely glad he should have written it; it is a contribution to our knowledge of what can be done—or what cannot. Ivan Turgenev has written a tale about a deaf and dumb serf and a lap-dog, and the thing is touching, loving, a little masterpiece. He struck the note of life where Gustave Flaubert missed it—he flew in the face of a presumption and achieved a victory.

Nothing, of course, will ever take the place of the good old fashion of "liking" a work of art or not liking it: the most improved criticism will not abolish that primitive, that ultimate test. I mention this to guard myself from the accusation of intimating that the idea, the subject, of a novel or a picture, does not matter. It matters, to my sense, in the highest degree, and if I might put up a prayer it would be that artists should select none but the richest. Some, as I have already hastened to admit, are much more remunerative than others, and it would be a world happily arranged in which persons intending to treat them should be exempt from confusions and mistakes. This fortunate condition will arrive only, I fear, on the same day that critics become purged from error. Meanwhile, I repeat, we do not judge the artist with fairness unless we say to him, "Oh, I grant you your starting-point, because if I did not I should seem to prescribe to you, and heaven forbid I should take that responsibility. If I pretend to tell you what you must not take, you will call upon me to tell you then what you must take; in which case I shall be prettily caught. Moreover, it isn't until I have accepted your data that I can begin to measure you. I have the standard, the pitch; I have no right to tamper with your flute and then criticize your music. Of course I may not like your idea at all; I may think it silly, or stale, or unclean; in which case I wash my hands of you altogether. I may content myself with believing that you will not have succeeded in being interesting, but I shall, of course, not attempt to demonstrate it, and you will be as indifferent to me as I am to you. I needn't remind you that there are all sorts of tastes: who can know it better? Some people, for excellent reasons, don't like to read about carpenters; others, for reasons even better, don't like to read about courtesans. Many object to Americans. Some readers don't like quiet subjects; others don't like bustling ones. Some enjoy a complete illusion, others the consciousness of large concessions. They choose their novels accordingly, and if they don't care about your idea they won't, *a fortiori*, care about your treatment."

So that it comes back very quickly, as I have said, to the liking: in spite of M. Zola, who reasons less powerfully than he represents, and who will not reconcile himself to this absoluteness of taste, thinking that there are certain things that people ought to like, and that they can be made to like. I am quite at a loss to imagine anything (at any rate in this matter of fiction) that people ought to like or dislike. Selection will be sure to take care of itself, for it has a constant motive behind it. That motive is simply experience. As people feel life, so they will feel the art that is most closely related to it. This closeness of relation is what we should never forget in talking of the effort of the novel. Many people speak of it as a factitious, artificial form, a product of ingenuity, the business of which it is to alter and arrange the things that surround us, to translate them into conventional, traditional moulds. This, however, is a view of the matter which carries us but a very short way, condemns the art to an eternal repetition of a few familiar clichés, cuts short its development, and leads us straight up to a dead wall. Catching the very note and trick, the strange irregular rhythm of life, that is the attempt whose strenuous force keeps fiction upon its feet. In proportion as in what she offers us we see life without rearrangement do we feel that we are touching the truth; in proportion as we see it with rearrangement do we feel that we are being put off with a substitute, a compromise and convention. It is not uncommon to hear an extraordinary assurance of remark in regard to this matter of rearranging, which is often spoken of as if it were the last word of art. Besant seems to me in danger of falling into the great error with his rather unguarded talk about "selection." Art is essentially selection, but it is a selection whose main care is to be typical, to be inclusive. For many people art means rose-colored windowpanes, and selection means picking a bouquet for Mrs. Grundy. They will tell you glibly that artistic considerations have nothing to do with the disagreeable, with the ugly; they will rattle off shallow commonplaces about the province of art and the limits of art until you are moved to some wonder in return as to the province and the limits of ignorance. It appears to me that no one can ever have made a seriously artistic attempt without becoming conscious of an immense increase—a kind of revelation—of freedom. One perceives in that case—by the light of a heavenly ray—that the province of art is all life, all feeling, all observation, all vision. As Besant so justly intimates, it is all experience. That is a sufficient answer to those who maintain that it must not touch the sad things of life, who stick into its divine unconscious bosom little prohibitory inscriptions on the end of sticks, such as we see in public gardens—"It is forbidden to walk on the grass; it is forbidden to touch the flowers; it is not allowed to introduce dogs or to remain after dark; it is requested to keep to the right." The young aspirant in the line of fiction whom we continue to imagine will do nothing without taste, for in the case his freedom would be of little use to him; but the first advantage of his taste will be to reveal to him the absurdity of the little sticks and tickets. If he has taste, I must add, of course he will have ingenuity, and my disrespectful reference to that quality just now was not meant to imply that it is useless in fiction. But it is only a secondary aid; the first is a capacity for receiving straight impressions.

Besant has some remarks on the question of "the story" which I shall not attempt to criticize, though they seem to me to contain a singular ambiguity, because I do not think I understand them. I cannot see what is meant by talking as if there were a part of a novel which is the story and part of it which for mystical reasons is not—unless indeed the distinction be made in a sense in which it is difficult to suppose that any one should attempt to convey anything. "The story," if it represents anything, represents the subject, the idea, the *donnee* of the novel; and there is surely no "school"—Besant speaks of a school—which urges that a novel should be all treatment and no subject. There must assuredly be something to treat; every school is intimately conscious of that. This sense of the story being the idea, the starting-point, of the novel, is the only one that I see in which it can be spoken of as something different from its organic whole; and since in proportion as the work is successful the idea permeates and penetrates it, informs and animates it, so that every word and every punctuation-point contribute directly to the expression, in that proportion do we lose our sense of the story being a blade which may be drawn more of less out of its sheath. The story and the novel, the idea and the form, are the needle and thread, and I never heard of a guild of tailors who recommended the use of the thread without the needle, or the needle with the thread. Besant is not the only critic who may be observed to have spoken as if there were certain things in life which constitute stories, and certain others which do not. I find the same odd implication in an entertaining article in the *Pall Mall Gazette*, devoted, as it happens, to Besant's lecture. "The story is the thing!" says this graceful writer, as if with a tone of opposition to some other idea. I should think it is, as every painter who, as the time for "sending in" his picture looms in the distance, finds himself still in quest of a subject—as every belated artist not fixed about his theme will heartily agree. There are some subjects which speak to us and others which do not, but he would be a clever man who should undertake to give a rule—an index expurgatorius—by which the story and the no-story should be known apart. It is impossible (to me at least) to imagine any such rule which shall not be altogether arbitrary. The writer in the *Pall Mall* opposes the delightful (as I suppose) novel of Margot la Balafree to certain tales in which "Bostonian nymphs" appear to have rejected English dukes for "psychological reasons." I am not acquainted with the romance just designated, and can scarcely forgive the *Pall Mall* critic for not mentioning the name of the author, but the title appears to refer to a lady who may have received a scar in some heroic adventure. I am inconsolable at not being acquainted with this episode, but am utterly at a loss to see why it is a story when the rejection (or acceptance) of a duke is not, and why a reason, psychological or other, is not a subject when a cicatrix is. They are all particles of the multitudinous life with which the novel deals, and surely no dogma which pretends to make it lawful to touch the one and unlawful to touch the other will stand for a moment on its feet. It is the special picture that must stand or fall, according as it seems to possess truth or to lack it. Besant does not, to my sense, light up the subject by intimating that a story must, under penalty of not being a story, consist of "adventures." Why of adventures more than of green spectacles? He mentions a category of impossible things, and among them he places fiction without adventure. Why without adventure, more than without matrimony, or celibacy, or parturition, or cholera, or hydropathy, or Jansenism? This seems to me to bring the novel back to the hapless little role of being an artificial, ingenious thing—bring it down from its large, free character of an immense and exquisite correspondence with life. And what is adventure when it comes to that, and by what sign is the listening pupil to recognize it? It is an adventure—an immense one—for me to write this little article; and for a Bostonian nymph to reject an English duke is an adventure only less stirring, I should say, than for an English duke to be rejected by a Bostonian nymph. I see dramas within dramas in that, and innumerable points of view. A psychological reason is, to my imagination, an object adorably pictorial; to catch the tint of its complexion—I feel as if that idea might inspire one to Titianesque efforts. There are few things more exciting to me, in short, than a psychological reason, and yet, I protest, the novel seems to me the most magnificent form of art. I have just been reading, at the same time, the delightful story of *Treasure Island*, by Robert Louis Stevenson, and, in a manner less consecutive, the last tale from M. Edmond de Goncourt, which is entitled *Cherie*. One of these works treats of murders, mysteries, islands of dreadful renown, hairbreadth escapes, miraculous coincidences, and buried doubloons. The other treats of a little French girl who lived in a fine house in Paris, and died of wounded sensibility because no one would marry her. I call *Treasure Island* delightful, because it appears to me to have succeeded wonderfully in what it attempts; and I venture to bestow no epithet upon *Cherie*, which strikes me as having failed deplorably in what it attempts—that is, in tracing the development of the moral consciousness of a child. But one of these productions strikes me as exactly as much of a novel as the other, and as having a "story" quite as much. The moral consciousness of a child is as much a part of life as the islands of the Spanish Main, and the one sort of geography seems to me to have those "surprises" of which Besant speaks quite as much as the other. For myself (since it comes back in the last resort, as I say, to the preference of the individual), the picture of the child's experience has the advantage that I can at successive steps (an immense luxury, near to the "sensual pleasure" of which Besant's critic in the *Pall Mall* speaks) say Yes or No, as it may be, to what the artist puts before me. I have been a child in fact, but I have been on a quest for a buried treasure only in supposition, and it is a simple accident that with M. de Goncourt I should have for the most part to say No. With George Eliot, when she painted that country with a far other intelligence, I always said Yes.

The most interesting part of Besant's lecture is unfortunately the briefest passage—his very cursory allusion to the "conscious moral purpose" of the novel. Here again it is not very clear whether he be recording a fact or laying down a principle; it is a great pity that in the latter case he should not have developed his idea. This branch of the subject is of immense importance, and Besant's few words point to considerations of the widest reach, not to be lightly disposed of. He will have treated the art of fiction but superficially who is not prepared to go every inch of the way that these considerations will carry him. It is for this reason that at the beginning of these remarks I was careful to notify the reader that my reflections on so large a theme have no pretension to be exhaustive. Like Besant, I have left the question of the morality of the novel till the last, and at the last I find I have used up my space. It is a question surrounded by difficulties, as witness the very first that meets us, in the form of a definite question, on the threshold. Vagueness, in such a discussion, is fatal, and what is the meaning of your morality and your conscious moral purpose? Will you not define your terms and explain how (a novel being a picture) a picture can be either moral or immoral? You wish to paint a moral picture or carve a moral statue: will you not tell us how you would set about it? We are discussing the Art of Fiction; questions of art are questions (in the widest sense) of execution; questions of morality are quite another affair, and will you not let us see how it is that you find it so easy to mix them up? These are things so clear to Besant that he has deduced from them a law which he sees embodied in English fiction, and which is "a truly admirable thing and a great cause for congratulation." It is a great cause for congratulation indeed when such thorny problems become as smooth as silk. I may add that in so far as Besant perceives that in point of fact English fiction has addressed itself preponderantly to these delicate questions he will appear to many people to have made a vain discovery. They will have been positively struck, on the contrary, with the moral timidity of the usual English novelist; with his or with her aversion to face the difficulties with which on every side the treatment of reality bristles. He is apt to be extremely shy (whereas the picture Besant draws is a picture of boldness), and the sign of his work, for the most part, is a cautious silence on certain subjects. In the English novel (by which of course I mean the American as well), more than in any other, there is a traditional difference between that which people know and that which they agree to admit that they know, that which they see and that which they speak of, that which they feel to be a part of life and that which they allow to enter into literature. There is the great difference, in short, between what they talk of in conversation and what they talk of in print. The essence of moral energy is to survey the whole field, and I should directly reverse Besant's remark and say not that the English novel has a purpose, but that it has a diffidence. To what degree a purpose in a work of art is a source of corruption I shall not attempt to inquire; the one that seems to me least dangerous is the purpose of making a perfect work. As for our novel, I may say lastly on this score that as we find it in England today it strikes me as addressed in a large degree to "young people," and that this in itself constitutes a presumption that it will be rather shy. There are certain things which it is generally agreed not to discuss, not even to mention, before young people. That is very well, but the absence of discussion is not a symptom of the moral passion. The purpose of the English novel—"a truly admirable thing, and a great cause for congratulation"— strikes me therefore as rather negative.

There is one point at which the moral sense and the artistic sense lie very near together; that is in the light of the very obvious truth that the deepest quality of a work of art will always be the quality of the mind of the producer. In proportion as that intelligence is fine will the novel, the picture, the statue partake of the substance of beauty and truth. To be constituted of such elements is, to my vision, to have purpose enough. No good novel will ever proceed from a superficial mind; that seems to me an axiom which, for the artist in fiction, will cover all needful moral ground: if the youthful aspirant take it to heart it will illuminate for him many of the mysteries of "purpose." There are many other useful things that might be said to him, but I have come to the end of my article, and can only touch them as I pass. The critic in the *Pall Mall Gazette*, whom I have already quoted, draws attention to the danger, in speaking of the art of fiction, of generalizing. The danger that he has in mind is rather, I imagine, that of particularizing, for there are some comprehensive remarks which, in addition to those embodied in Besant's suggestive lecture, might without fear of misleading him be addressed to the ingenuous student. I should remind him first of the magnificence of the form that is open to him, which offers to sight so few restrictions and such innumerable opportunities. The other arts, in comparison, appear confined and hampered; the various conditions under which they are exercised are so rigid and definite. But the only condition that I can think of attaching to the composition of the novel is, as I have already said, that it be sincere. This freedom is a splendid privilege, and the first lesson of the young novelist is to learn to be worthy of it. "Enjoy it as it deserves," I should say to him; "take possession of it, explore it to its utmost extent, publish it, rejoice in it. All life belongs to you, and do not listen either to those who would shut you up into corners of it and tell you that it is only here and there that art inhabits, or to those who would persuade you that this heavenly messenger wings her way outside of life altogether, breathing a superfine air, and turning away her head from the truth of things. There is no impression of life, no manner of seeing it and feeling it, to which the plan of the novelist may not offer a place; you have only to remember that talents so dissimilar as those of Alexandre Dumas and Jane Austen, Charles Dickens and Gustave Flaubert have worked in this field with equal glory. Do not think too much about optimism and pessimism; try and catch the color of life itself. In France today we see a prodigious effort (that of Emile Zola, to whose solid and serious work no explorer of the capacity of the novel can allude without respect), we see an extraordinary effort, vitiated by a spirit of pessimism on a narrow basis. M. Zola is magnificent, but he strikes an English reader as ignorant; he has an air of working in the dark; if he had as much light as energy, his results would be of the highest value. As for the aberrations of a shallow optimism, the ground (of English fiction especially) is strewn with their brittle particles as with broken glass. If you must indulge in conclusions, let them have the taste of a wide knowledge. Remember that your first duty is to be as complete as possible—to make as perfect a work. Be generous and delicate and pursue the prize."

Critical Remarks on Hawthorne's *Twice-Told Tales*

Edgar Allan Poe

Originally published in *Graham's Magazine* in 1842, Poe's essay on Hawthorne's tales is widely considered to be the first piece of modern short story criticism and theory. It is credited with bringing a new seriousness to the study of the short story as a form. Poe argued that the story should receive serious critical consideration because "the tale proper affords unquestionably the fairest field for the exercise of the loftiest talent, which can be afforded by the wide domains of mere prose." The main thrust of his theory is that, in a successful tale, "the unity of effect or impression is a point of the greatest importance." This idea was central to the composition of his own tales as well as his poems, and continues to influence current study and writing of short stories. Not all critics, however, have shared Poe's enthusiasm for the relentless pursuit of effect. W. C. Brownell, in his famous essay on Poe's work (also in this volume), while acknowledging that Poe's "most noteworthy success is the completeness of his effect," nevertheless criticizes the narrative atmosphere this completeness creates, "an atmosphere which is less the envelope than the content of his work, and which so enwraps the detail as to blend its accents and minimize the force of such variety as it has." Brownell's criticism touches on the great debate that has continued to torment Poe's reputation for more than a century: Was he in fact no more than a master of sing-song lyrics and predictably suspenseful prose in the most usual gothic mode, or was he the literary genius who best dramatized, in both poetry and fiction, the darkest recesses of the fledgling American psyche?

The book professes to be a collection of *tales,* yet is, in two respects, misnamed. These pieces are now in their third republication, and, of course, are thrice-told. Moreover, they are by no means *all* tales, either in the ordinary or in the legitimate understanding of the term. Many of them are pure essays; for example, "Sights from a Steeple," "Sunday at Home," "Little Annie's Ramble," "A Rill from the Town Pump," "The Toll-Gatherer's Day," "The Haunted Mind," "The Sister Years," "Snow-Flakes," "Night Sketches," and "Foot-Prints on the Sea-Shore." We mention these matters chiefly on account of their discrepancy with that marked precision and finish by which the body of the work is distinguished.

Of the essays just named, we must be content to speak in brief. They are each and all beautiful, without being characterized by the polish and adaptation so visible in the tales proper. A painter would at once note their leading or predominant feature and style it *repose.* There is no attempt at effect. All is quiet, thoughtful, subdued. Yet this repose may exist simultaneously with high originality of thought; and Hawthorne has demonstrated the fact. At every turn we meet with novel combinations; yet these combinations never surpass the limits of the quiet. We are soothed as we read; and withal is a calm astonishment that ideas so apparently obvious have never occurred or been presented to us before. Herein our author differs materially from Lamb or Hunt or Hazlitt—who, with vivid originality of manner and expression, have less of the true novelty of thought than is generally supposed, and whose originality, at best, has an uneasy and meretricious quaintness, replete with startling effects unfounded in nature, and inducing trains of reflection which lead to no satisfactory result. The essays of Hawthorne have much of the character of Irving, with more of originality, and less of finish; while, compared with the *Spectator*, Irving, and Hawthorne have in common that tranquil and subdued manner which we have chosen to denominate *repose*; but, in the case of the two former, this repose is attained rather by the absence of novel combination, or of originality, than otherwise, and consists chiefly in the calm, quiet, unostentatious expression of commonplace thoughts. In them, by strong effort, we are made to conceive the absence of all. In the essays before us the absence of effort is too obvious to be mistaken, and a strong undercurrent of *suggestion* runs continuously beneath the upper stream of the tranquil thesis. In short, these effusions of Hawthorne are the product of a truly imaginative intellect, restrained and in some measure repressed, by fastidiousness of taste, by constitutional melancholy and by indolence.

But it is of his tales that we desire principally to speak. The tale proper, in our opinion, affords unquestionably the fairest field for the exercise of the loftiest talent, which can be afforded by the wide domains of mere prose. Were we bidden to say how the highest genius could be most advantageously employed for the best display of its own powers, we should answer, without hesitation—in the composition of a rhymed poem, not to exceed in length what might be perused in an hour. Within this limit alone can the highest order of true poetry exist. We need only here say, upon this topic, that, in almost all classes of composition, the unity of effect or impression is a point of the greatest importance. It is clear, moreover, that this unity cannot be thoroughly preserved in productions whose perusal cannot be completed at one sitting. We may continue the reading of a prose composition, from the very nature of prose itself, much longer than we can persevere, to any good purpose, in the perusal of a poem. This latter, if truly fulfilling the demand of the poetic sentiment, induces an exaltation of the soul which cannot be long sustained. All high excitements are necessarily transient.

Thus a long poem is a paradox. And, without unity of impression, the deepest effects cannot be brought about. Epics were the offspring of an imperfect sense of art, and their reign is no more. A poem too brief may produce a vivid, but never an intense or enduring impression. Without a certain continuity of effort—without a certain duration or repetition of purpose—the soul is never deeply moved. There must be the dropping of the water upon the rock. DeBeranger has wrought brilliant things—pungent and spirit-stirring—but, like all impassive bodies, they lack *momentum,* and thus fail to satisfy the poetic sentiment. They sparkle and excite, but, from want of continuity, fail deeply to impress. Extreme brevity will degenerate into epigrammatism, but the sin of extreme length is even more unpardonable. *In medio tutissimus ibis.*

Were we called upon, however, to designate that class of composition which, next to such a poem as we have suggested should best fulfill the demands of high genius—should offer it the most advantageous field of exertion—we should unhesitatingly speak of the prose tale, as Hawthorne has here exemplified it. We allude to the short prose narrative requiring from a half-hour to one or two hours in its perusal. The ordinary novel is objectionable, from its length, for reasons already stated in substance. As it cannot be read at one sitting it deprives itself, of course, of the immense force derivable from *totality*. Worldly interests intervening during the pauses of perusal, modify, annul, or counteract, in a greater or less degree, the impressions of the book. But simple cessation in reading, would, of itself, be sufficient to destroy the true unity. In the brief tale, however, the author is enabled to carry out the fullness of his intention, be it what it may. During the hour of perusal the soul of the reader is at the writer's control. There are no external or extrinsic influences—resulting from weariness or interruption.

A skillful literary artist has constructed a tale. If wise, he has not fashioned his thoughts to accommodate his incidents; but having conceived, with deliberate care, a certain unique or single effect to be wrought out, he then invents such incidents—he then combines such events as may best aid him in establishing this preconceived *effect*. If his very initial sentence tend not to the outbringing of this effect, then he has failed in his first step. In the whole composition there should be no word written, of which the tendency, direct or indirect, is not to the one pre-established design. And by such means, with such care and skill, a picture is at length painted which leaves in the mind of him who contemplates it with a kindred art, a sense of the fullest satisfaction. The idea of the tale has been presented unblemished, because undisturbed; and this is an end unattainable by the novel. Undue brevity is just as exceptionable here as in the poem; but undue length is yet more to be avoided.

We have said that the tale has a point of superiority even over the poem. In fact, while the *rhythm* of this latter is an essential aid in the development of the poet's highest idea—the idea of the beautiful—the artificialities of this rhythm are an inseparable bar to the development of all points of thought or expression which have their basis in truth. But truth is often, and in very great degree, the aim of the tale. Some of the finest tales are tales of ratiocination. Thus the field of this species of composition, if not in so elevated a region on the mountain of mind, is a table-land of far vaster extent than the domain of the mere poem. Its products are never so rich, but infinitely more numerous, and more appreciable by the mass of mankind. The writer of the prose tale, in short, may bring to his theme a vast variety of modes or inflections of thought and expression—(the ratiocinative, for example, the sarcastic, or the humorous) which are not only antagonistical to the nature of the poem, but absolutely forbidden by one of its most peculiar and indispensable adjuncts; we allude, of course, to rhythm. It may be added here, *par parenthèse*, that the author who aims at the purely beautiful in a prose tale is laboring at great disadvantage. For beauty can be better treated in the poem. Not so with terror, or passion, or horror, or a multitude of such other points. And here it will be seen how full of prejudice are the usual adversions against those *tales of effect*, many fine examples of which were found in the earlier numbers of *Blackwood*. The impressions produced were wrought in a legitimate sphere of action, and constituted a legitimate although sometimes an exaggerated interest. They were relished by every man of genius: although there were found many men of genius who condemned them without just ground. The true critic will but demand that the design intended be accomplished, to the fullest extent, by the means most advantageously applicable.

We have very few American tales of real merit—we may say, indeed, none, with the exception of *The Tales of a Traveler* of Washington Irving, and these *Twice-Told Tales* of Hawthorne. Some of the pieces of John Neal abound in vigor and originality; but in general, his compositions of this class are excessively diffuse, extravagant, and indicative of an imperfect sentiment of art. Articles at random are, now and then, met with in our periodicals which might be advantageously compared with the best effusions of the British magazines; but, upon the whole, we are far behind our progenitors in the department of literature.

Of Hawthorne's *Tales* we would say, emphatically, that they belong to the highest region of art—an art subservient to genius of a very lofty order. We had supposed, with good reason for so supposing, that he had been thrust into his present position by one of the impudent *cliques* which beset our literature, and whose pretensions it is our full purpose to expose at the earliest opportunity; but we have been most agreeably mistaken. We know of few compositions which the critic can more honestly commend than these *Twice-Told Tales*. As Americans, we feel proud of the book.

Hawthorne's distinctive trait is invention, creation, imagination, originality—a trait which, in the literature of fiction, is positively worth all the rest. But the nature of originality, so far as regards its manifestation in letters, is but imperfectly understood. The inventive or original mind as frequently displays itself in novelty of *tone* as in novelty of matter. Hawthorne is original at *all* points.

It would be a matter of some difficulty to designate the best of these tales; we repeat that, without exception, they are beautiful. "Wakefield" is remarkable for the skill with which an old idea—a well-known incident—is worked up or discussed. A man of whims conceives the purpose of quitting his wife and residing *incognito*, for twenty years, in her immediate neighborhood. Something of this kind actually happened in London. The force of Hawthorne's tale lies in the analysis of the motives which must or might have impelled the husband to such folly, in the first instance, with the possible causes of his perseverance. Upon this thesis a sketch of singular power has been constructed.

"The Wedding Knell" is full of the boldest imagination—an imagination fully controlled by taste. The most captious critic could find no flaw in this production.

"The Minister's Black Veil" is a masterly composition of which the sole defect is that to the rabble its exquisite skill will be *caviare*. The *obvious* meaning of this article will be found to smother its insinuated one. The moral put into the mouth of the dying minister will be supposed to convey the *true* import of the narrative, and that a crime or dark dye (having reference to the "young lady") has been committed, is a point which only minds congenial with that of the author will perceive.

"Mr. Higginbotham's Catastrophe" is vividly original and managed most dexterously.

"Dr. Heidegger's Experiment" is exceedingly well imagined, and executed with surpassing ability. The artist breathes in every line of it.

"The White Old Maid" is objectionable, even more than the "Minister's Black Veil," on the score of its mysticism. Even with the thoughtful and analytic, there will be much trouble in penetrating its entire import.

"The Hollow of the Three Hills" we would quote in full, had we space—not as evincing higher talent than any of the other pieces, but as affording an excellent example of the author's peculiar ability. The subject is commonplace. A witch subjects the Distant and the Past to the view of a mourner. It has been the fashion to describe, in such cases, a mirror in which the images of the absent appear; or a cloud of smoke is made to arise, and thence the figures are gradually unfolded. Hawthorne has wonderfully heightened his effect by making the ear, in place of the eye, the medium by which the fantasy is conveyed. The head of the mourner is enveloped in the cloak of the witch, and within its magic folds there arise sounds which have an all-sufficient intelligence. Throughout this article also, the artist is conspicuous—not more in positive than in negative merits. Not only is all done that should be done, but (what perhaps is an end with more difficulty attained) there is nothing done which should not be. Every word tells, and there is not a word which does *not* tell.

In "Howe's Masquerade" we observe something which resembles plagiarism—but which *may be* a very flattering coincidence of thought. The idea here is, that the figure in the cloak is the phantom or reduplication of Sir William Howe; but in an article called "William Wilson," one of the *Tales of the Grotesque and Arabesque*, we have not only the same idea but the same idea similarly presented in several respects.

Here it will be observed that, not only are the two general conceptions identical, but there are various *points* of similarity. In each case the figure seen is the wraith or duplication of the beholder. In each case the scene is a masquerade. In each case the figure is cloaked. In each, there is a quarrel—that is to say, angry words pass between the parties. In each the beholder is enraged. In each the cloak and sword fall upon the floor. The "villain, unmuffle yourself," of Mr. H. is precisely paralleled in a passage of "William Wilson."

In the way of objection we have scarcely a word to say of these tales. There is, perhaps, a somewhat too general or prevalent *tone*—a tone of melancholy and mysticism. The subjects are insufficiently varied. There is not so much of *versatility* evinced as we might well be warranted in expecting from the high powers of Hawthorne. But beyond these trivial exceptions we have really none to make. The style is purity itself. Force abounds. High imagination gleams from every page. Hawthorne is a man of the truest genius. We only regret that the limits of space will not permit us to pay him that full tribute of commendation, which, under other circumstances, we should be so eager to pay.

On Poe

William Crary Brownell

William Crary Brownell, in this essay on the place of Edgar Allan Poe in American and world literature, attributes Poe's endurance as a literary figure more to Poe's "pronounced individuality" than to literary achievement of high quality. Poe is important, says Brownell, because it is through his fiction and poetry that "Romantic art entered the portals of our literature and illuminated its staid precincts." This is largely the extent of his praise, for when it comes to the matter of individual works, Brownell finds much lacking in Poe's productions. While acknowledging that, "as a technician [Poe's] most noteworthy success is the completeness of his effect," one of Brownell's main criticisms is that Poe, in his perfection of technique, ultimately affects only the "nerves," and not the intellects, of his readers, creating an unsatisfying literary experience. (For an alternate view, see Poe's own remarks on his theory of effect in his essay on Hawthorne's *Twice-Told Tales*, also in this volume.) Ultimately, in Brownell's view, the emphasis upon technique and effect results in "an atmosphere which is less the envelope than the content of his work, and which so enwraps the detail as to blend its accents and minimize the force of such variety as it has." Poe's desire to manipulate his readers by assaulting their senses with images of the horrible is "the delight of degenerates," not the goal of a true literary artist.

This, of course, is one opinion of Poe and his work. Where Brownell sees gratuitous terror and predictability, other critics find a clever thrill and originality of construction. Those other critics might also detect the influence of a personal agenda in Brownell's attacks. Still, the primary value of Brownell's study of Poe is in the minute consideration of Poe's narrative strategy—how Poe, as an author of a certain type of tale and poem, seeks to create a response in his readers, and how his approach compares to others in effectiveness and literary quality.

I

There is no more effective way of realizing the distinction of Poe's genius than by imagining American literature without him. One is tempted to add there is no other way. It is in the historic rather than in the critical estimate that his eminence appears. It owes more to its isolation than to its quality. He was extremely individual, the entire character of his mind and nature is acutely, almost painfully, certainly perversely, personal; but his originality appears chiefly in relief against the background of his environment. If he did not feel intensely, he thought energetically, but to a purport more familiar in older societies than in our own. His figure acquires outline and edge from its contrast with the prevailing Philistine screen which he sedulously kept behind it and on which he made it the business of his life to cast the sharpest possible shadow. He was from the first in complete disaccord with his environment and lived in a perpetual state of warfare with it. His parentage was bohemian, his childhood and youth dependent, his associations—in the half savage, half aristocratic society of his boyhood—expressly favorable to the development of the imperious beneficiary whose sense of his own powers and of his lack of claims brought him through a rather irregular and not very grateful adolescence to the threshold of a manhood of revolt. There is a whole literature of revolt in older countries. Our only Ishmael is Poe. But if not unprecedented in the history of letters he was sufficiently salient among us, and the fact that so generally his hand was against every man accentuated his individuality in the natural course of apology and polemic.

The established was with us still the moral and the didactic. Poe's antagonism instinctively inclined him to art. He is in fact the solitary artist of our elder literature. This is his distinction and will remain such. Hawthorne is in a degree a rival, but in *form*, as his addiction to allegory attests, and in any case his Puritan preoccupation with the moral forces invalidates his purely aesthetic appeal. Poe's art was unalloyed. It was scrupulously devoid, at any rate, of any aim except that of producing an effect and often overspread if only occasionally clothed with the sheen of beauty. As such it was in America at the time an exotic. His great service to his country is in a word the domestication of the exotic. Color, rhythm, space, strangeness, were his "reals"—they fascinated his mind and took possession of his else unoccupied soul. In the large sense thus his art is in strictness to be called exotic rather than original. French, German, and English Romanticism had preceded him. He pillaged and plagiarized freely. In the matter of literary phase, his most convinced admirer and most thorough-going apologist observes that he came at the close of an epoch, he did not introduce one. But in his hands the method and even the material that he adopted resulted in a very striking body of work, which still has the compactness and definition of a monument. And if he contributed little he passed on the torch. Incarnated in the vivid forms his pronounced individuality imagined, illustrated by the energy of his genius, the spirit of Romantic art entered the portals of our literature and illuminated its staid precincts to the end of variety at the very least. Whatever has responsibility for the subsequent riot there, her vivifying influence is clear, and for it we are indebted to Poe.

II

The artist, by definition, exercises his activity in exclusive concentration upon his effect. In so far as his attention swerves from that he modifies his distinctive attitude. He may, for instance, forget his effect in the rapture of expression and rise to poetry. But unless, in so doing, his sub-consciousness at least keeps its hold on his effect—as, for example, Tennyson's always did—he prelimits his purely artistic function. This is why, in a world of imperfections, the most nearly perfect act is so often the least satisfactory—assuming the poetic to be the ultimate standard; why the perfection of Vermeer fades before the irregularities of Rembrandt; why we turn from Veronese to Tintoretto; why in only an occasional miracle of genius like Raphael at his best do we find a stable fusion of spirit and statement; why—to descend from august illustration—readers more sensitive to art than to poetry are deceived by the poetic disguise of that errant artist, Walt Whitman, who achieved a fairly radiant degree of perfection in never yawping his commonplaces off the key, in spite of the variety of their modulations. Like Whitman's, Poe's attention never wandered a moment from his effect—even in his poetry. Now the effect in poetry, as in any fine art, is largely a matter of technique, and a great deal of poetry is naturally overvalued, because it answers the technical test, because in short it sounds good.

In the first place its technique is so difficult that, when it is achieved with any distinction, it is rewarded with at least the temporary appreciation that inevitably rewards the tour de force. The technical test has in truth a good deal to say for itself practically. Winckelmann objected to artists' criticism of art that it naturally made difficulty overcome the test of achievement. But as a matter of fact, one may ask, is not this at least one test, since it is clearly one source of the superiority of the superior artist, whose laurels, without it, would be worn equally by the mute and the inglorious, not to say the manifestly incompetent? What one can say is that it is in no sense the test of the artist's inspiration, and that this is, after all, the main thing. The difficulties of the art of poetry, at any rate, are sufficiently attested by the abounding surplusage of unsuccessful attempts to surmount them. Everyone accordingly—except apparently the deluded practitioner—is struck by the exceptional victory when he encounters it, and apt unconsciously to ascribe to inspiration the effect really due to energy and skill, forgetting that even inspired skill is not poetic inspiration. Much of the admiration of Poe's poetry is of this kind. Much of his poetry itself can be admired in no other way.

Moreover, the technique of poetry is so multifarious, so full of possibilities, so capable of producing pleasure by mere rhyme and rhythm that with many readers at all times and with all readers at some times its content is lost sight of. English literature has a wonderful example of this in the poetry of Swinburne. Swinburne is incomparable, but Poe has something—a tithe—of the same richness of rhythmic resource, though his numbers are artificial at times and at times tenuous to a degree that removes them from even superficial classification with the opulent spontaneity and splendor of the English poet's diction. They are, too, though less richly, more exclusively, technical, leaning thus all the more heavily on technique. And his technique, being thus the main factor of his verse, lacks a little the native felicity only to be secured by keeping it in its true relative position. Forced out of its proper subordination it loses its grace as a contributing element of a larger entity. It, instead of the subject, being the poet's main concern, its theoretic quality becomes obvious. It acquires a positively notional air with Poe at times—the air of illustrating the notions of his negligible "Philosophy of Composition" and "The Poetic Principle." Its resources seem devices. Every effect seems due to an expedient. The repetend and the refrain are reliances with him—not instrumental, but thematic. At least they constitute rather than create the effect—which has therefore something perfunctory about it.

Technique of all sorts interested Poe tremendously. He had what might be called the technical temperament—a variety perhaps more familiar than widely recognized. It is the temperament that delights in terminology, labels, little boxes and drawers, definitions, catalogues, categories, all ingeniously, that is to say mechanically, opposite and perfectly rigid. It illustrates the activity of mind avoiding the drudgery of thought by definiteness of classification. Manner being more susceptible of classification than matter, how the thing is done interests it more than the thing itself. Such a temperament on larger lines than common, with a certain sweep as well as system, Poe possessed. It rose to the pitch of positive genius with him. He pondered, himself, and lectured his contemporaries on how literature should be written, how a tale should be presented, how a poem should be built up. His criticism is largely, almost exclusively, technical. He pursued it quite in the detective spirit. His review of "Barnaby Rudge," of which to Dickens' amazement he divined the denouement, is worthy of M. Dupin and is historic. His long criticisms of Cooper and Hawthorne are craftsman's criticism. And as such they are extraordinarily good. They contrast refreshingly with the general run of literary praise and blame in his day—and in ours—in being specific, pointed and competent and avoiding the vague, the sentimental and the commonplaces of moralizing, though of course they have none of the overtones, so to say, of either culture or philosophic depth that enrich criticism as well as give it a creative value. His own craftsmanship considered strictly as such is excellent. He proceeds with perfect self-possession and deliberation; and there is this to be said for his philosophizings about it, that at least they disclosed his own method and show conclusively that his art was an art of calculation and not the spontaneous expression of a weird and gruesome genius that it seems to so many upon whom it produces its carefully prepared effect.

His theory of poetry is stated within his account of the composition of "The Raven" which is as a whole probably in no better faith than the anonymously published editorial reference to the poem that accompanied it on its appearance.

Both are mystifications which if "The Raven" were finer would tend to vulgarize it, and are only saved, by being possibly derisory, from being actually as risible as Browning found the poem itself. But the theory advocated and illustrated by Poe is undoubtedly as sincere as his perverse pursuit of originality at any cost, and his temperamental revolt against what is staple and standard, not to speak of what is classic, would permit. It is briefly that poetry has absolutely nothing to do with truth, (to which he had an intellectual repugnance) that it is concerned solely with beauty (which he does not define, but assumes, in opposition to more conventional opinion from Plato to Keats, to be absolutely divorced from truth), and that its highest expression is the note of sadness—the sadder the better. Of these notions only the last need arrest attention. It is true that the most perfect beauty has often the note of sadness. The reason probably resides rather in its effect than in its constitution, being largely the recipient's subjective appreciation reacting even in, or especially in, the presence of perfection which contrasts so bitterly with

"—the heavy and the weary weight
Of all this unintelligible world."

But it is not true that this is always the case. Who is to decide, for example, between the "Ode to a Nightingale" and the "Ode on Immortality?" Poe's theory, however, and its elaborate working out, involve the inference that "The Raven" is a finer poem than either, since Wordsworth's ode is actually joyous, and the idea of "The Raven" on the other hand sadder than anything in Keats'. He proves it by *a plus b*: Of all melancholy topics, he says, death is the most melancholy; it is most poetical when it allies itself with beauty; "the death then of a beautiful woman is unquestionably the most poetical topic in the world."

Any force his theory might abstractly be supposed to have assuredly evaporates in his illustrative exposition of it, and "The Raven" is certainly superior to either. But two things are made perfectly clear by such theorizing: one, that the theorist is primarily not a poet but an artist—concerned less with expression than with effect, that is to say; and, the other, that he is not a natural but an eccentric artist, since sadness voluntary and predetermined is artificial and morbid. The poem itself—undoubtedly Poe's star performance—confirms these inductions. It is not a moving poem. It has, as Elizabeth Browning herself admitted, a certain power, but it is such power as may be possessed by the incurable dilettante coldly caressing a morbid mood. To be moving melancholy must be temperamental. Even a mood will not suffice. "The Raven" is in conception and execution exceptionally cold-blooded poetry. But, distinct on the plane of artifice, it is admirable art. Less remarkable as a pure tour de force in linguistic luxuriance than the extraordinary "Bells," which in its way is quite unparalleled, it is nevertheless a noteworthy technical achievement. Its rhythms and rhymes are more than clever and together with the recurrent accent of the refrain—already used by Lowell—combine in the production of a sustained tone and effect of totality, which may almost be said to epitomize Poe's genius.

Both "The Raven" and "The Bells" have enjoyed an enormous popularity among readers impressionable by effects and insensitive to distinctions, and their poetic strain has not saved them from being the natural prey of the professional elocutionist—also an elaborate technician in his more or less humble fashion. Poe's more personal verse has less interest. Some of it deserves Stoddard's verdict of "doggerel," for where his own work, verse or prose, was concerned he had no standard. The lines "For Helen" written when he was a boy are not only astonishingly precocious but charming, far better than those "For Annie" written when he had matured and for the most part overlaid his inspiration with artistry and encrusted it with technique. The idea and inspiration of "The Haunted Palace," however, amply sustain the happy technical art that expresses them with not only admirable musical aptness, but with a beautiful fusion of restraint born of taste and ease springing from fullness that makes it an indisputable masterpiece. Its reserve, indeed, secures an objectivity that is exceptional in Poe and, since his art was fundamentally more genuine than his inspiration, exceptionally moving. For once he got himself out of the way and let his genius guide him to complete success. "The Conqueror Worm" is less successful, I think, in being more a tour de force. It shares a little the "staginess" of the *donnee* and his taste shows its fickleness by deserting him, though it is certainly a spirited piece of pessimism and—no slight praise—the last two lines are among the classics of the "catching." On the other hand in "Ulalume" one feels the sincerity latent in the most artificial and abnormal natures—though a sincerity that throws into sharper relief than usual the element of artifice in Poe's art and seems itself in the shadow that perhaps befits remorse, behind the apparatus of repetend and empty assonance that tries the reader's nerves. Even here one feels the aptness of Emerson's bland reference to him (in conversation with Howells) as the "jingle man," and notes the artist rather than the poet and the technician rather than the artist. In any case the volume of his verse is so slight as to confine his claim to its quality, and its quality is, in general, hardly such as to place him very high up on the fairly populous slopes of Parnassus where there is more competition than he met with in his lifetime. Competition is fatal to Poe. His cue was distinctly to function outside of it and he was wise to cultivate originality at any price.

III

As a technician his most noteworthy success is the completeness of his effect. He understood to perfection the value of tone in a composition, and tone is an element that is almost invaluable. In this respect he has no American and few foreign rivals. All of his writings attest his supreme comprehension of it—prose as well as poetry, the ablest and the most abject. Such rubbish as "The Duc de l'Omelette" with its galvanic rictus of false but sustained gaiety; such elaborate and hollow solemnity as the parable "Shadow," which ends, however, on a note of real pith and dignity, such a crazy-quilt of tinsel as "The Assignation," all have this unifying quality which makes art of them. His very deficiency in the qualities usually present in the romance writer and absolutely vital in romance of a high order, enabled him to cultivate his own special excellence the more exclusively. Many of the tales are tone and nothing else—not even tone of any particular character but a reticulation of relations merely in admirable unison. The false note is the one falsity he eschewed. Tinkling feet on a tufted carpet is nonsense, but it is not a false note in the verbal harmony of the artificial "Raven." In "The Cask of Amontillado" the tone is like the click of malignant castanets. And in "The Fall of the House of Usher" it reaches Poe's climax of power—a diapason of gloom, wholly voluntary, and ending none too soon perhaps, but maintained to the end with the success of a veritable tour de force. What on the other hand he did not understand was modulation. He has no variety. Probably he realized this limitation and confined himself almost wholly in prose to the short story, and, grotesquely, to one hundred lines as the limit of a poem. A novel by Poe is inconceivable, and would be even if he had had the feeling for character and the human interest that the novel demands. This is partly because he lacked sustained power, and the larger art of organization and dynamic development, but it is also due to the monotony that results probably from the predominance and prolongation of the mood, which makes it so easy for him to secure tone.

Thus he achieves atmosphere but an atmosphere which is less the envelope than the content of his work, and which so enwraps the detail as to blend its accents and minimize the force of such variety as it has. Nothing takes place in "The Fall of the House of Usher" that is not trivial and inconclusive compared with its successful monotone, its atmosphere of lurid murk and disintegrating gloom. And as a consequence of this inversion of the normal artistic relations of content and envelope I must say I think that even here, where we have Poe at his best, he refuses us all satisfaction that lies beyond the scope of purely scenic art. In this one respect "The Cask of Amontillado" is better. It, too, is most remarkable artistically for its tone, the cascade of brilliant chatter that sustains its suspense. But it contains some psychology, devilish rather than human, to be sure, and therefore as usual ringing false, yet imaginatively thrilling in its malignity, though its monstrousness is rendered somewhat insipid by the perversity and characteristic inadequacy of its motive. And it has a situation both moral and material and a rapidly conducted, however meager, action. But even these two tales as they stand do not take their author out of the rank of the purely scenic artist, comparatively high as they may place him within it. The truth is that no writer of anything approaching Poe's ability has been content to remain in this rank.

There is unquestionable power in his best tales, but it is a repellent power. Its manifestations are either unsympathetic or repulsive—unsympathetic where successful because they make their effect by attacking instead of charming the sensibilities, repulsive where they fail because nothing but success can excuse such sinister assault. The mental attitude of the reader who cooperates with a writer so systematically bent on his conquest instead of on his captivation is singularly innocent. And I do not think the experienced share it. Mainly, I imagine, Poe's stories are read in youth and rarely returned to—except by patriotic critics of a tendency to dithyramb, and too solicitous to magnify the salient figures of our literature to reconsider their own early evaluations. A mature judgment must discern, and a mature susceptibility resent, the writer's manifest motive. In fact his most characteristic limitation as an artist is the limited character of the pleasure he gives. He has a perverse instinct for restricting it to that produced by pain. Pain and pleasure have no doubt an equivalent aesthetic sanction. Metaphysically they are sometimes, indeed, difficult to distinguish; desire, for example, which superficially classes itself as pleasure being probably pain in reality. The discussion of such a question would have delighted Poe; but it is unnecessary to quarrel with the legitimacy of painful effects in art—in which, as in life no doubt, as Browning declared, "pain is not the fruit of pain"—in order to appreciate the perversity of Poe's practice in this regard. The production of pain is with him an end, not a means to the production of pleasure. His design is, crassly, to wring the withers of our sensoriums. Such a design is the delight of the degenerate. Decadents, such as Baudelaire, discern it readily and naturally—or unnaturally, as one chooses—savor it and enjoy to the full "the generous pleasure of praising" it. The naive and hearty and good natured and uncritical with a weakness for the romantic at any price, such as Gautier, fail to note it and admire its results as revolutionary simply. Doubtless nothing would have surprised him more, and more evoked his scorn, than the assertion that such a foe to philistinism as himself lacked ideality. He had ideality but it was exclusively artistic. It was entirely consistent with unscrupulousness. No doubt the most loathsome subjects are susceptible of artistic treatment and may serve the ends of beauty. But a preference for them in the artist raises a presumption against his competence in the circumstances—a presumption amply justified in Poe's case. Not whatsoever things are lovely and of good report, but whatsoever things are effective were his preoccupation. Intensity of effect was accordingly his end, and artifice his means. And fine things are not thus produced. The law of the universe in virtue of which the beautiful, the true, and the good are inextricably interrelated forbids it. Matthew Arnold maintained that it was "lost labor" to inquire into a writer's motive. Undoubtedly errors have been made by allowing the real or supposed springs of a writer's production to color one's appreciation of them. Thackeray's view of Sterne, for example, is rather summary. But with Poe the case is different. The only reason for its being lost labor to inquire into his motive is the fact that his motive is in plain sight. And to neglect it would be to neglect what not only colors, but is the constituent element of a large portion—a large proportion indeed—of his writings.

In the most characteristic this motive is exactly that of the fat boy in "Pickwick" who announced to his easily thrilled auditors that he was going to make their flesh creep. To accomplish this result, however, is more difficult than to announce it, unless one deals with an altogether higher order of material than Poe's, and is possessed of an altogether different order of powers. The element of awe is not, of course, in question, and there is no need to cite more august examples than that of Victor Hugo, for instance, to remind ourselves by contrast of the difference between the flesh-creeping effects produced by a master and those obtained by a charlatan who addresses not in the last the mind, but exclusively the nerves. In fact the comparison of any great writer to Poe, it may be incidentally remarked, results in the sense of contract, and would undoubtedly instinctively be called unfair by his admirers, many of whom "do not," as the phrase is, "know very well what they want." His success in accomplishing his desired effect at all events is fatally compromised, usually, in two ways: his motive is too plain and his means are too primitive. He makes his motive so plain, not only by its constant undisguised and obvious recurrence, but by actual profession (see "The Philosophy of Composition" and "The Poetic Principle," for example) as to defeat its own end. It is impossible to meet halfway an artist whose efforts to surprise, shock, startle you are all the while in full sight. He must perforce forego the unconscious reciprocity of concern that is the essence of appreciation. A writer who declares at every turn, as the inveteracy of Poe's practice, his constant harping on the string of "horror," declares, that he is "going to make your flesh creep" can hardly succeed in doing so. In the face of such an announcement any flesh at all jaded by the extravagances of Romanticism remains stationary. In the case of some of Poe's stories, in fact, positive paralysis ensues in the face of almost hysterical efforts on his part at galvanism— "The Pest" for instance. For this carnomaniac purpose, too, his means are as primitive as his motive is plain. He can certainly produce his effect when the material he treats is of a nature to produce it in anyone's hands. The subject itself of "The Premature Burial" is full of horror, and can be trusted to come home to the imagination of the reader under any treatment of it. So with the idea of being walled up alive as presented in "The Cask of Amontillado." So also with the situation in "The Pit and The Pendulum." But in most instances it may certainly be said that one does not get enough pain out of Poe to receive any great amount of pleasure from him.

He carries his "unscrupulousness" very far indeed—much farther than even in Arnold's estimation Kinglake could be said to! In fact, if throughout his work you feel the artist, you also feel the artistic liar. He is the avatar of the type—a type tolerably well known in a multitude of examples from Mandeville to Munchausen and establishing perhaps through its mere existence, if anything could, the absence of any necessary connection between art and truth. Truth stood between him and originality. It irked him equally in pursuing the egregious, in which he delighted, and in eluding the commonplace, which he abhorred. The esoteric attracted, and the ecumenical repelled him. He was fascinated by the false as Hawthorne was by the fanciful. He was, as Henry Martin said, "always in revolt against the despotism of fact." He was an artist in whom the great purpose of art, making the unreal appear real, became the end of making the false appear true. At this flagitious game he evinced the superior cleverness of the children of this world. Nowhere is his skill more noteworthy than in securing verisimilitude for the improbable, the incredible, one of the most obvious of his expedients being the auto-biographical form, for which he shows the notorious partiality of the so-called habitual liar. I have not made the calculation, but I should think there were not a half dozen of his sixty-eight tales in which this form is not employed, and these are not among his comparatively few successes; when the material is extraordinary this personal presentation of it gives it great plausibility in the esteem of the credulous, though it is to be said that it arouses a corresponding distrust in the skeptical. The same fondness for the false appears in his occasional inversion of the process, whereby the truth is made to seem incredible—marvelous beyond belief, "too good to be true," in a word, but true all the same. Here of course the falsity of effect merely takes the place of falsity of material. It was all one to Poe, provided he satisfied his passion for mystification. The shortest road to producing the sensational effect that alone he sought is to controvert the established order and for that road apart from its being the line of least resistance he had a native affinity. The key-note indeed of his nature is revolt.

In instinctive recalcitrancy to the general constitution of things he passed his life in kicking against its pricks and produced his literature in the process. Inevitably the false, the ugly and the wrong attracted him, since the established standard is of the good, the beautiful and the true. But as the established is the only conceivable standard he was naturally forced to treat the former trinity in conjunction with, if not in terms of, the latter. The effect he aimed at being exclusively a sensational effect, he could best secure it by falsifying his material, and thus circumventing the reader's tranquillity of expectation. The fact that such sensation is valueless was of no concern to a philosopher who attached value to sensation as such and to sensation only. Hence he devoted the powers of an extraordinary intellect to producing what is to the intellect of next to no interest. The abnormal, in its various manifestations, the sinister, the diseased, the deflected, even the disgusting were his natural theme. He would not conceive the normal save as the commonplace for which he had apparently the "horror" he would have liked to inspire in others by the presentation of the eccentric. Dread of the commonplace, as was pointed out centuries ago by a far otherwise penetrating critic than Poe, is fatal to the sublime. And there is assuredly no sublimity in Poe.

Yet the tales of horror and those of the weird and the fantastic probably stand in the widest popular estimate as especially characteristic. And it is true that it is of these one thinks when one speaks of a Poe story. They have, many of them, the evil eminence that willful morbidity lends to the production of its votaries of genius, and except for the effect on the nerves which a few of them are able to produce on "suggestible" sensoriums, they hold their place among other writings of a similar sort—there are none precisely like them, because of their meagerness—chiefly on account of their scenic quality. More has been claimed for the "tales of ratiocination" as they are called. Writers before Poe have "groveled in the ghastly and wallowed in the weird" with considerable effect if with an art inferior to his. But he has been called the inventor of the detective story, and thus decorated with a badge of unique distinction in the hierarchy of literature. It is always difficult to assign with certainty to any individual the invention of a literary or plastic genre. "Doubtless Homer had his Homer," remarks Thoreau. M. Dupin was certainly preceded by *Zadig*, and Voltaire is said to have invented *Zadig* after reading an Oriental prototype. And even ascribing to Poe the invention of the detective story, the lover of literature may justly exclaim, "la belle affaire!" and feel disposed rather to charge than to credit him with it. However, to start or even accelerate a literary current of magnitude, whatever its merit, is an accomplishment so rare as to be noteworthy on that account alone. And though it is, no doubt, the detective story that is most indebted to him in this respect, it is by no means the only fruit of his remarkable inventiveness. "No man," says a writer in the London Spectator, "struck out so many new lines in the region of romance," and he proceeds to derive Jules Verne's stories from "Hans Pfall," "She" from "A. Gordon Pym," "Treasure Island" from "The Gold Bug," "Dr. Jekyll and Mr. Hyde" from "William Wilson," Zola, Flaubert's and even H. G. Wells' realism from Poe's minute detail, etc. This does not of course modify his own conclusion that "it is an inhuman and perverse judgment that finds in Poe the springs of truly great writing," and it should also be pointed out that there is a considerable element of fancifulness—the fancifulness of the literal—in such romantic etymology. It is quite conceivable that neither Jules Verne nor Stevenson, nor Rider Haggard nor any of the other writers in question was conscious of any specific or general indebtedness to Poe, whom also in the different genres in question, save perhaps that of "The Gold Bug," they one and all altogether surpassed. Wells, for example, might excusably prefer to derive his mystification from the minute detail of Swift. Nevertheless, such analogies are eloquent witness of Poe's inventive genius—characterize, in fact, his genius as inventive rather than imaginative.

For that reason he seems to me, as I began by saying, more personal than truly original in the higher literary sense, since, though he was extremely idiosyncratic, nevertheless what he originated lay definitely in the sphere of invention. His imaginative writing is far less original. Having the imaginative in mind we may say that originality consists in taking a fresh view, originating a new conspectus, a new synthesis, of life and the world—turning objective material around a little and exhibiting it with a different silhouette. It is in this way that real contributions to literature are made, and it is thus that the really great writer serves literature as the savant advances science. There is nothing of this kind to be looked for in Poe. The true material of literature he left precisely where he found it, for all his fantastic stirring of it and uneasy striving with it. On the lower plane of invention, his mechanical and mathematical turn, his fecundity in ideas, conceptions, experimental notions certainly devised new modes, new fashions as it were, in fiction—which, indeed, was precisely what he himself understood by the originality he pursued and declared universally attainable. And in this field "ratiocination" is distinctly his forte. Here he excelled if he did not, narrowly speaking, invent; or rather, broadly speaking, excelled as well as invented. In this respect "The Gold Bug" is probably an unsurpassed masterpiece; a masterpiece, at any rate—which is no doubt eulogy enough, though M. Lemaitre's characterization of Maupassant as "*a peu pres irreproachable dans un genre qui ne l'est pas*," is certainly applicable to it. So in a less degree is "The Murders in the Rue Morgue." "The Purloined Letter" is decidedly inferior and "The Mystery of Marie Roget" quite unworthy of the inventor of the detective story. In "The Purloined Letter" the effect of M. Dupin's contemptuousness dominates that of his skill, and in "The Mystery of Marie Roget" the arrogance of the author is destructive of all interest in a tale that is also otherwise tedious. When Poe's personality comes to the surface the effect is always unpleasant, and it is the absence of temperamental color that gives an agreeable relief to such exhibitions of his purely intellectual activity as "The Gold Bug" and "The Murders in the Rue Morgue," just as among his weird and fantastic tales the best are those in which there are the most evidences of his art and the fewest of his disposition.

However, the extraordinary disproportion of inferior work in his prose does not obscure the fact that he was essentially an artist. The fact that there are hardly a dozen good ones among his sixty-eight tales is not due to any deflection of his artistic attitude. He had no other attitude—save that of necessity involved in his contentous exposition of artistic principles and his temperamental reprobation of practitioners of a different turn. Polemically he certainly shows little of the detachment so often prescribed to the artist. But even in polemic whenever he is in the least impersonal and disinterested it is the artistic for which he is contending. He is not averse to "abusing the plaintiff's attorney," but the plaintiff's case he attacks on artistic grounds. Even in his poorer work, even in his poorest, the workmanship is always the best element. It is poor enough in some of it, but in such tales as "Four Beasts in One," "Loss of Breath," "The Man that was Used Up," "Never Bet the Devil Your Head," in fact almost all the "tales of extravaganza and caprice," there is assuredly nothing else. In such inexplicable "extravaganzas" as "The Duc de l'Omelette" and "Lionizing" its stark salience gets on one's nerves. The excessive predominance of this kind of thing in his tales is due obviously to failure in inspiration. But more obscurely it is undoubtedly due to alcohol. "Bon-Bon," for example, seems definitely characteristic of inebriety. The effect of alcohol is well known to be the relief of that tension which the maintenance of equilibrium imposes so painfully on such organizations as Poe's, and a consequence of excessive indulgence in it is therefore the loss of that balance of the faculties which secures correct judgments. It is impossible to account for much of Poe's writing except on the theory that both in conception and in execution it was in this way transfigured to his mind and sense. He saw it through the mist of mental congestion and saw in its incoherence the significance that escapes sobriety. Even his egotism would be insufficient otherwise to explain it. The effects of opium in stimulating and coloring the poetic imagination—as in Coleridge's case—are familiar. But those of alcohol are pathologically quite different and quite inferior, and it does not seem to have been sufficiently remarked that in Poe's case they were undoubtedly responsible for the deterioration of his literary productions as well as for the pathetic disintegration of his life. It is a generous instinct that shrinks from dwelling on the latter, but the naivete that ignores the obvious origin of much of his "extravaganza and caprice" is less generous than blind—and above all slightly ridiculous. The explanation at all events seems to reduce *ad absurdum* the sanction of being "thrilled" for the "thrill's" sake.

IV

The truth is it is idle to endeavor to make a great writer of Poe because whatever his merits as a literary artist his writings lack the elements not only of great, but of real, literature. They lack substance. Literature is more than an art. It is art in an extended sense of the term. Since it is the art that deals with life rather than with appearances it is the art *par excellence* that is art plus something else—plus substance. Its interest is immensely narrowed when it can only be considered plastically—narrowed to the point of inanity, of insignificance. Poe was certainly an artist, but the fact that he was exclusively an artist and an artist in an extremely restricted sense, of itself minimizes the literature he produced. Shakespeare, for example, is neither exclusively nor supremely an artist. M. Jules Lemaitre informs us how much better in some respects—in artistic respects—Racine would have written "Hamlet." Every art of course, has its conventions. It rearranges them from time to time, it is subject to the law of evolution, but it depends on them always. And in so far as literature is an art it, too, leans upon them. It has its schools, its phases, its successive points of view, its academic perfections, its solecisms. But the fact that it deals with life itself rather than exclusively with appearances—which may be arranged, organized, systematized, controlled far more easily through their greater preliminary simplification—gives it so much more range, so much greater freedom, such an infinitely greater miscellaneity of material of so much more significance and vitality, that is comparatively independent of conventions, and finds its supreme justification in giving anyhow, in any way, well or ill one may almost say, the effect of life, the phenomena and significance of life which constitute its substance. Thus it is that in literature substance counts so much more than it counts in any other art, however much any other may also be in its degree "a criticism of life." Henry James has curiously illustrated the principle in later years. Beginning as pre-eminently or at least conspicuously an artist he has become so overwhelmed by the prodigious wealth and miscellaneity of his material—that is to say, the phases of life which his prodigious penetration has revealed to him—that his art has been submerged by it. The trees have obliterated the forest. All the more important is it, one may argue, to cling to conventions of treatment, that your picture of life may be definite, coherent and effective. Yes, but one of these conventions is a certain correspondence with reality. Life being the subject of literature more fully and directly than it is of any purely plastic art that deals with appearances— which are necessarily more ordered and adaptable and in a sense art themselves, or a stage of it—being indeed the substance as well as the subject of literature, this correspondence with reality is exacted by it of any treatment of it that is, even as art, to have any interest or value. The doctrine of art for art's sake applied to literature is apt to have particularly insipid results.

In short, however extravagant and capricious, any work of art is necessarily subject to its material and the hand of every artist must like the dyer's be subdued to what it works in. But a literary composition, especially, cannot be conceived and executed *in vacuo*. The warp must be "given," however wholly the woof may be invented, or the web will be insubstantial and the pattern incoherent. Poe could transact his imaginings in environments of the purest fancy, in no-man's land, in the country of nowhere, and fill these with "tarns" and morasses and "ragged mountains" and shrieking water-lilies, flood them with ghastly moonlight and aerate them with "rank miasmas." Nevertheless, he could only avoid the flatness of pure phantasmagoria by peopling them with humanity. His landscape might embody extravagance and his atmosphere enshroud caprice, but his figures demanded to be made human. The overwhelming interest of fiction is its human interest. Since it is peopled with human figures neglect of its population is a contradiction in terms. Even in the fiction of adventure, in which the personages are minimized and the incidents the main concern, even in fiction in which plot figures as the protagonist of the drama, plot and incident would be sterile but for the characters that figure in them. However subordinate and undifferentiated these may be, they must make some intrinsic appeal, or we should not care what happened to them. The game even as a game is not one that can be played with counters. Yet, that is precisely the way in which Poe played it. And his stories have no human interest because humanity did not in the least interest him. Neither man nor woman delighted him enough to occupy his genius even incidentally. His tales contain, of course, no "character"—that prime essential, and most exacting *raison d'etre* of normal fiction. But what is surprising is the absolute inhumanity of the personages he is compelled to incarnate and the absolutely inhuman way in which he sets them forth. In almost every case of importance, as I have said, the chief personage is the narrator and—perhaps a little from this substantially unvaried practice, though mainly, I think, because of the real resemblance—the narrator suggests Poe himself. Each is very baldly the center of his universe. The two take pretty much the same view—an astonishingly external one so far as human nature is concerned. The illusion of the story is subserved, but of the story quite apart from the personages. What it gains in illusion, it loses in significance. Indeed, so great is the importance of human character to a story that deals with it at all that I think those of Poe's tales in which the personages are the least shadowy, the least like algebraic symbols, the least characteristic, that is to say, are greatly helped by the fact. The stories in which he figures gain greatly from M. Dupin, who has a pedantic and censorious temperament though his differentiation is as inferior to that of his successor, M. Lecoq, as the meager and mathematical medium in which he exists is to the varied and entertaining field of activity, full of character and crowded with incident, that Gaboriau furnished for the latter—without, however, reaching eminence as a "world-author" in the process. "The Fall of the House of Usher" gains greatly from the characters therein, though these are merely sketches for the reader's imagination to fill out. One thinks of "Wuthering Heights" and of the place in literature that would have been assigned to Emily Bronte by Poe admirers, had she had the good fortune to be born an American. "The Pit and the Pendulum," one of the best of the tales, it seems to me, owes much to its exceptional "psychology" as an imaginative study of real torture to which ingenuity gives real point instead of merely displaying itself as ingenuity. It is helped, too, I think, by being localized in real time and space; by the fact that there was such an institution as the Inquisition, a fabric also quite otherwise "thrilling" than any of Poe's imagination, and that the victim's rescuers had an actual and the correct nationality, though I fear these considerations would seem philistine indeed to the true Poe worshipper. Furthermore, "The Murders in the Rue Morgue" forfeits a large part of its interest, the moment it appears that the murderer is an ape and not a human malefactor. *Ce n'est que ca*, one feels like exclaiming—and repeating even when William Wilson's double dissolves into his conscience, though of course allegorically that is the point of the story, as well as being very cleverly, very ingeniously, managed. Finally one of the tales—"The System of Dr. Tarr and Dr. Fether"—has an exceptional interest because it is an intelligent, though it does not pretend to be a profound, study of a phase of mind and character under certain conditions and in a certain environment, executed with a wholly unaccustomed lightness of touch and an aspect of gaiety. The scene, however, it will be remembered, is a *maison de sante* and the personages are its inmates. And nothing is more characteristic of Poe's perversity than that his most normal fiction should be the representation of the abnormal. The abnormal was essential to him, and he only varied his practice of achieving it in his treatment by securing it in his material. Taken with the whim of depicting human nature he could at least select its deflected types. Even here, however, his interest is clearly in treating his material in a rather ghastly vein of contrasting and contraindicated *bouffe*. He cares nothing for his "types," and his real success, such as it is, is incidental.

Similarly with his preoccupation with crime—almost an obsession with him. He is never concerned with sin, which is too integrally human an element of life to interest him. Crime on the contrary is in comparison of an artificial nature, and of however frequent still of exceptional occurrence. Undoubtedly it furnishes apposite material to the novelist of character as well as to the portraitist of manners, and is a personal as well as a social factor in human life. But this aspect of it Poe, whose criminals are only criminals, completely ignores. He uses it not naturalistically but conventionally. It is his conventional machinery for his story. Like Mme. Tussaud and Jarley he finds in it the readiest instrument of his most cherished effects. And so far as he "psychologizes" it he increases its inherent artificiality by treating it with morbid imaginativeness, endeavoring after his favorite method to give the illusion of reality to its abnormal repellency, and not at all concerned about demonstrating its real character. Here he is measurably successful in such a tale as "The Imp of the Perverse" where he utilizes the well known tendency of the criminal to confess, and totally fails in such absurdity as "The Black Cat," a story that could hardly have "thrilled" Ichabod Crane; but one illustrates his lack of human feeling as well as the other. And of almost all the stories into which the element of humanity enters perforce, it may be said, finally, that the residuum is not so much worth while as to earn neglect of his shortcomings in a respect normally vital to the kind of thing he is doing. In a word the "Poe" in his stories could only be moving and effective, if this element were present also.

For the only thing that can give any significance, any vital interest, any value, in a word, to the weird and the fantastic themselves is to establish them somehow in some human relationship—as Hoffmann does. Otherwise they are simply phenomena that appeal strictly to the nerves. Poe's treatment of them negates their sole sanction. "He can thrill you as no one else can," says one of his admirers. As to that there are several things to be said. In the first place it depends a good deal on who you are whether you are "thrilled" or not. In the next place how are you "thrilled?" As you are by the knocking at the door in Macbeth, or as you are by a bad dream or a gruesome sight in actual life? Thirdly, are you thus affected because the story is thrilling, or because, as I have already noted, your own imagination is set at work as to how you would be affected by experiencing what you are reading of— "The Premature Burial" for example—forgetful of the fact that personal application, than which nothing is more common, notoriously vitiates any objective judgment. Finally of what value after all is "gooseflesh" as a guide to correct estimates in art? Is this hyperaesthetic reaction a trustworthy measure of real aesthetic merit? To ask these questions is of course to answer them. But even accepting this effect on the nerves as evidence of Poe's power, even of his unique power—for I think no other writer ever essayed it so baldly—its essential insignificance must be admitted because it is wholly divorced from any element of interest outside of itself. Instead of itself being an element in a composition, as with Hoffmann, Poe's weirdness is the whole thing. An occasional discord has its uses in a work of harmony, but the shriek of a locomotive performs no function but that of irritation, though it may "thrill" or even deafen a listener. It is certainly more important to be moved than to be moved pleasantly, but to be moved to no purpose, to be agitated aimlessly in no direction, is an unsatisfactory experience.

It is needless to specify instances among Poe's tales that illustrate this exclusive appeal to the nerves. It would be difficult to find any among those of the weird class that do not. Besides, in them it was his theory, his "scheme," to create this precise effect and no other. The particularly crass one of "Berenice" however shows his method in particular relief. It is that product of his genius in which a madman recounts his fascination by the beautiful teeth of his mistress and his exhumation of her remains for the purpose of extracting them as a last exercise of his faculties before losing these completely. Poe sometimes went too far and did so in this instance, as if it mattered where along that line one stopped. The partly ridiculous, partly repulsive, wholly inept quality of the performance is stamped as such at the start. The serious workmanship only emphasizes the fact that the personages are lay figures, the motif insane, the story incredible. As a ship-shape and coherent account of incoherent horror it may contain a "thrill" for the predisposed, but it is fully as fitted to wake a smile as a shudder and there is obviously no standard by which to admeasure this sort of thing except that of technical execution. Any reader of "Berenice" not a neurasthenic must inevitably ask, "What of it?" Having no import it has no importance.

V

"Berenice" epitomizes very well Poe's lack of substance and the insignificance of the fantastic element in his work which this lack of substance involves. It also illustrates the aridity of his imagination. Imagination is, in the view of most of his admirers, probably his most striking, his most salient possession. But it is darkening counsel to stop with this mere ascription as if imagination were an invariable rather than a protean faculty. Poe's imagination was of a peculiarly personal kind. It intensified his divining powers, but never extended his range of thought. It was thoroughly, integrally, analytic. His "Tales of Conscience," as they have been called, deal mechanically so far as they do not deal conventionally with conscience. There is no largely imaginative treatment of it. They summarize phenomena deduced from remorse and fear as forces and, confined to crime as they are, involve little imaginative psychology. His imaginings are largely inventive, and important as the imagination is to the inventor, the tendency to invention is apt to imply an inferior order of it. The poets are sadly lacking in the inventive faculty. It is essentially logical, concatenated, mechanical. It has no spiritual and no sensuous side. Poe's inventiveness is his chief mental trait and his imagination was its servant. He is perhaps at his best in "The Gold Bug"—to Poe's partisans a miracle of imaginative invention but only to his partisans anything else. His spiritual side is illustrated by his "Ligeias," "Eleanoras" and "Morellas"—which measured by a serious standard are scarcely more than morbid moonings. The ingenuity of his one spiritual tale, "William Wilson" is far more in evidence than its imaginativeness. It is an extremely artistic piece of workmanship and shows what Poe's art could do in the service to truth instead of mystification. But only up to the point when you perceive it is mystification after all. Curiously, then the effect deliquesces—when its meaning appears—with the entrance of avowed allegory. The whole thing becomes insubstantial because his imagination is unequal to conducting his fine conception to its conclusion without destroying his illusion. His sensuousness is distinctly rudimentary, all glitter and tinsel, ebony and silver. His consecration to beauty seems a little ironical in the light of his too frequent conception of it. Witness "The Assignation," with its "mingled and conflicting perfumes, reeking up from strange convolute censers, together with multitudinous flaring and flickering tongues of emerald and violet fire," its "thousand reflections from curtains which rolled from their cornices like cataracts of molten silver," its "beams of natural glory" which "mingled at length fitfully with the artificial light and lay weltering in subdued masses upon a carpet of rich, liquid-looking cloth of gold"—all of which *"richesse de cafe,"* as Balzac would call it, suggests Thackeray caricaturing Disraeli and Bulwer combined—those twin sources of Poe's style according to his latest editors who, however, must have been thinking only of its extravagances, as his style in general is admirable.

In any case such writing is not sensuous but scenic. And Poe had no more the sensuous than the sensual strain. The sensual as commonly understood does not exist for him, apparently, as it is apt not to in persons of his variety of nervous organization, and his writings it is to be pointed out have this signal negative merit. But he perhaps pays for it in some degree by an extraordinary aridity in the whole sensuous sphere. When he enters this he is either perfectly insignificant or else his taste deserts him. He is too insincere to succeed in it. His nature requires the element of the artificial which distinguishes the scenic. His genius was certainly a striking one and if he was a charlatan he certainly had a genius for charlatanry. He reveled in the specious. The vivid aspect of reality he gave to his creations is due to his skill in its use, for he never felt reality and was impervious to its appeal as the true constitution of the universe, moral and material. What he desired was to be striking. He says so in so many words in one of his disingenuous (or merely perverse, who knows?) argumentations, contending that any one can be original if he will. And his usual means of accomplishing it was by giving through speciousness the semblance of reality to the unreal and incredible. He relied on this far more than even on his scenic imagination, though his scenic imagination gave him great power of vivid material realization; his landscapes are stereoscopic. The scenic, however, demands scale. With Poe the scale is too small. His stage is lilliputian. He is so fond of the lime-light in itself that he floods his picture with it. But for the proper play of this illuminant more time and space are needed than his cabinet canvas contains. His imagination is not rich enough to engender extension, endue it with continuity and crowd it with action. His action is always meagre and, one may say, deduced from, rather than largely illustrative of, his idea. Or else it is conventional, as in the "Adventures of A. Gordon Pym" which is the acme of stereotyped "adventure," imitating even the religious outgivings of "Robinson Crusoe" with grotesquely mechanical effect.

On the other hand he was full of ideas. If he lacked the visualizing moral power of the image-making faculty, if his action and incidents are meagre and gain their aspect of reality through a specious art of presentation rather than by the actual incarnation of artistic vision, what eminently he did not lack was fertility in intellectual conception. Sixty-eight stories, whatever their average quality, are a good many. His picture might be vague, but it never lacked subject. He cannot be said to have lived in the world of ideas, in the accepted sense of the phrase, for he had but a smattering acquaintance with its established consensus. Predeterminedly original, however, he created his own. Artist as he was, he was nevertheless far more predisposed to the abstract than to the concrete, except in the purely material sphere; he began with principle and proceeded to phenomena, in irreproachably deductive fashion. Analytical as he was, he conducted his analysis deductively; he had a passion for ratiocination, but he argues synthetically. His conclusion is always his own point of departure—artistically withheld till the climax is reached in the verification of hypothesis. This is the difference between M. Dupin and the inductive Zadig, for example. He was tremendously concerned with theory, a circumstance that gives point to his criticism and coherence to his tales, however it may devitalize his poetry. His mind was highly speculative, inquiring, even inquisitional. He had a prodigious interest in problems, puzzles, rebuses—an interest that to those who do not share it is apt to seem inept. He was in a way a conjurer in literature. He delighted in mystification—which is as much as to say he had no other interest in mystery. He was less of a mystic than any writer who has ever dealt with the mysterious. He had vastly more affinity with Cagliostro than with Hoffmann from whom—inexplicably—he is so often said to derive. Without the vanity he had the conceit and enjoyed the complacence of the prestidigitator.

In his early studies, mathematics, and in his later reading, science in general, attracted him most genuinely. With all his gift for language it interested him mainly as syntax, and his knowledge of languages was as superficial as his care for letters. His French for example—which is not infrequent—is what he would censure in another as culpably ignorant. He may be said, indeed, to have indulged his mathematical turn in his philosophy of life—or whatever may serve to pass for it with him; of course as such he had no philosophy of life. His interest in ideas did not extend to moral ones, of which he had none. The whole world of morals was a terra incognita to him—not at all the same thing as saying, which is also true, that he had no morals. Coleridge, for example, has been said to have had none, but he was immensely concerned with their philosophy. Poe's personal egotism accentuated by his indulgence freed him from a sense of personal responsibility no doubt, but the singular thing about him as a writer is that man's moral nature made no appeal to his imagination. Morbid psychology, to be sure, was a part of his material, but he used it almost altogether as a means mainly mechanical to the production of a dramatic effect. And even here his general ideas have not the scope and freedom they have in the purely intellectual sphere, but evince the succinct specific quality that marks the "notation" of phenomena. So that even his determination to the abnormal does not in the unfamiliar moral sphere remark any law of general import—except such commonplaces as the tendency of the criminal to confession already noted. And of course, as regards morals in the extended sense, he had, about man's habits and customs, around which the imagination of the normal literary artist plays perpetually, no ideas at all, either general or otherwise.

In brief, his lack of moral imagination accounts for the vacuity of his writings. A writer's product is characterized in great part by what he lacks as well as by what he possesses, by his defects as well as by his qualities. It is no reproach to a theological writer to be ignorant of the fine arts unless he refers to them. On the other hand it would be an insufficient characterization of a landscape painter to say that he could paint clouds if he could not paint trees, though certainly if he painted clouds extraordinarily well, that would be the most important thing to say about him, as it would signalize his contribution to landscape art, besides which his failure in any respect would be more negligible. The theory of criticism, however, which holds that the excellences of a performance are alone worth attention, that it is, unlike a rope, to be judged only by its strongest part, and that the function of criticism is really the judicial dispensing of rewards of merit, is unsatisfactory and provincial. The whole work is there calling for critical account and, due attention paid to the matter of emphasis and accent, its sins both of commission and omission are germane to critical consideration. In practice the other theory leads to notorious confusion and—as Americans at least must be constantly reminded—the distinction between good and bad is obscured by mechanically ascribing to a failure the characteristics of a performer's successes. At all events it is pertinently illuminating to find a writer of tales, criticism and poetry deficient in the philosophy of life, letters and feeling, not only because this at once ranks his product and measures its value, but on account of the light it throws on his productive faculty itself—his imagination. It is a just reproach to Hawthorne that he suffered the genius that produced "The Scarlet Letter" to produce little or nothing else comparable with it. But the case is quite different with Poe, because tales, criticism and poetry of real value cannot be written or can only occasionally be written with Poe's equipment. The wonder is not that he did not succeed more often, but that he succeeded at all, as assuredly he did in his own way—one can hardly say his own genre, since he had no congeners.

It is a mistake to try to classify him. He is very strictly *sui generis*. So appalling an egoist could hardly fail to be. No more superficial association was ever made than in relating him to Hoffmann, in whom the weird and the fantastic are always in close and generally in affectionate companionship with sentiment and humor. "Where form dominates" says

Balzac, "sentiment disappears," and in the temperament of the technician humor has as little place as sentiment. Notoriously Poe had none of either. He was an artist with a controlling bent toward artifice, exaggeratedly theoretic, convinced that the beautiful is the strange and the sad the poetic, and exercising his imagination through every expedient of ingenious invention, to the end of producing effects of strangeness to the point of abnormality and of sadness to the point of horror. Compact of neurotic sensationalism and saturated with the specious, Poe's "thrilling" tales taken in the mass illustrate the most detestable misuse of imaginative powers within the limits of serious literature, and only fall within these limits by the intellectual vigor which oftenest they argue rather than evince. "It's a weary feast," says Thackeray, "the banquet of wit where no love is." And Poe's banquet is as bereft of wit as it is destitute of love. He lacked humor and he lacked heart.

The Detective Story

Harry Thurston Peck

Peck's essay on detective fiction, or, what may be called better the fiction of reasoning, seeks to fulfill two goals: to establish detective stories as legitimate literary, and therefore artistic, objects, and, secondly, to give a critical treatment and comparison of some of the genre's major authors and their works in the context of his own useful definition of a successful detective tale. He wastes no time expressing his sentiments toward those who would exclude these stories from the category of literature—his dismissal of such opinions as "supercilious" is stated boldly in his opening sentence. Once he establishes the literariness of his objects, Peck goes on to discuss the function of the character of Watson in Arthur Conan Doyle's Sherlock Holmes stories, the relationships among these tales and their forerunners, both American and international, and other issues important to the critical consideration of this genre. In the process he makes a great point of, and does the genre a great service by, going against the contemporary critical grain; that is, he elevates such stories as the Sherlock Holmes tales where other critics would dismiss them as pulp (for another discussion of a critical iconoclast, see Cooper's essay on Ambrose Bierce, also in this volume).

Supercilious persons who profess to have a high regard for the dignity of "literature" are loath to admit that detective stories belong to the category of serious writing. They will make an exception in the case of certain tales by Edgar Allan Poe, but in general they would cast narratives of this sort down from the upper ranges of fine fiction. They do this because, in the first place, they think that the detective story makes a vulgar appeal through its exploitation of crime. In the second place, and with some reason, they despise detective stories because most of them are poor, cheap things. Just at present there is a great popular demand for them; and in response to this demand a flood of crude, ill-written, sensational tales comes pouring from the presses of the day. But a detective story composed by an author of talent, not to say of genius, is quite as worthy of admiration as any other form of novel. In truth, its interest does not really lie in the crime which gives the writer a sort of starting point. In many of these stories the crime has occurred before the tale begins; and frequently it happens, as it were, off the stage, in accordance with the traditional precept of Horace.

The real interest of a fine detective story is very largely an intellectual interest. Here we see the conflict of one acutely analytical mind with some other mind which is scarcely less acute and analytical. It is a battle of wits, a mental duel, involving close logic, a certain amount of applied psychology, and also a high degree of daring on the part both of the criminal and the person who hunts him down. There is nothing in itself "sensational" in the popular acceptance of that word.

The reasoning, for instance, in Poe's story of "The Purloined Letter" would excite the admiration of a mathematician or of a student of metaphysics. In the same author's most famous story, "The Murders in the Rue Morgue," there are to be sure some details that are terrible to read—hideous traces of a monstrous crime; but these details are necessary. The perpetrator of the crime is not a human being, but an orangutan, and this fact compels a description of the inhuman and frightful manner in which the murders were committed. But in general, not only in Poe, but in Ponson du Terrail and Gaboriau and Boisgobey, and Conan Doyle, the evil deed which is the cause of the whole action is usually passed over lightly, and very often it is not a crime of violence. Indeed, the matter may turn out to be no crime at all, but simply a mysterious happening, which the quick-witted, subtle hero is called in to solve, as in Doyle's "The Man With the Twisted Lip," or the same author's slighter tale, "A Case of Identity."

Therefore, when we speak of the detective story, and regard it seriously, we do not mean the penny-dreadfuls, the dime-novels, and the books which are hastily thrown together by some hack-writer of the "Nick Carter" school, but the skillfully planned work of one who can construct and work out a complicated problem, definitely and convincingly. It must not be too complex; for here, as in all art, simplicity is the soul of genius. The story must appeal to our love of the mysterious, and it must be characterized by ingenuity, without transcending in the least the limits of the probable.

The origin of the detective story is to be found in Voltaire's clever romance, *Zadig*, which he wrote under peculiar circumstances. He had fallen out of favor with the French court, because he had intimated that some of the members of the royal circle were guilty of cheating at cards. This brought upon him the keen displeasure of the queen. He feared at any moment he might be arrested and imprisoned in the Bastille. Within the hour, almost, he had his carriage prepared, and hurried away at half-past one in the morning. Arriving at a little wayside inn, he sent a letter to the Duchess du Maine, begging her to hide him in her chateau until he had been pardoned. For a month he lived in two rooms, which she provided for him, behind barred shutters, and with candles burning day and night.

There Voltaire wrote and wrote continually in his cramped hand, while his valet copied the sheets which his master kept tossing upon the floor with the ink still wet upon them. At two o'clock in the morning, Voltaire would go softly down to where the duchess was awaiting him, and eat a little supper in her presence, amusing her by his brilliant talk. Then he would creep back to his prison, and, after a brief interval of sleep, would once again fall to writing. It was under these strange circumstances that he composed the miniature masterpiece of romance which he called *Zadig*. Zadig is a marvelous philosopher and acute observer. One passage in the story tells how he described to the Persian king's attendant a horse and a dog which had been lost, and which Zadig had never seen. Nevertheless, he was able, by his powers of observation, and from certain indications, not only to describe the dog—its sex, size, and condition—but to tell correctly what sort of a bit was in the horse's mouth, and with what sort of shoes the animal had been shod.

It should be noted that the suggestion of this story, "Le Chien et Le Cheval," was not original with Voltaire. The tale is found in a slightly different form in De Mailly's *Voyage et Adventures des Trois Princes de Sarendip*, which appeared in 1719, or twenty-eight years before *Zadig* was written, and was even rendered into English twenty-four years before Voltaire conveyed it. But careful investigation has shown that De Mailly himself was not the originator. His story professes to have been translated from the Persian, but was, in fact, taken from an obscure Italian writer, Cristoforo Armeno, whose book was printed in Venice in 1557, and translated into French as early as 1610. As a matter of fact, the episode with which we are all familiar in Voltaire has an Eastern ancestry which can be traced through Arabic, Turkish, and Persian literature, and Talmudic Hebrew, until the clue is lost in the mists of a remote past.

In all these tales occurs the same kind of deductive reasoning which plays so great a part in the best detective stories of modern times. Just as Voltaire derived his hint from De Mailly, so Poe, who was steeped in French literature, must have drawn from Voltaire the same idea which he so brilliantly developed in his story, "The Purloined Letter." It is interesting to remember that the scene of all three of Poe's most famous detective tales—"The Murders in the Rue Morgue," "The Purloined Letter," and "The Mystery of Marie Roget"—is laid in France.

As has been said elsewhere, no one has surpassed the ingenuity of Poe in the construction of these stories. It was noted, however, that one's admiration ends with the matter of his constructiveness and reasoning, and I ventured to say that the defect in all these tales lies in the fact that their author could not create a living, breathing character. His personages are nothing but abstractions. He moves them about like chessmen on a board, and we are interested, not in them, but in the problem with which they have to do.

In order that the detective story should be something more than mathematics applied to fiction—or, perhaps, fiction applied to mathematics—it was necessary that what Poe did should be combined with a sympathetic understanding of human nature. This combination was effected—imperfectly, to be sure, but still with great ability—by Emile Gaboriau in the best of his detective novels, *M. Lecoq*.

Gaboriau was a journalist before he turned a novelist; and as a journalist he came to be interested in the problems with which the police of Paris had to deal. This was under the Second Empire, when Napoleon III, for his own personal safety, had established a marvelously elaborate system of espionage. The police records contained the daily history of almost every human being within the boundaries of France. Enrolled in the organization were not merely the usual police, but a host of unknown spies. These might apparently be shopkeepers, janitors, laborers, or whatever else seemed best; but apart from their ordinary occupations, they were the eyes and ears of the men who controlled them all at the central prefecture of police or the mysterious Black Room in the Tuileries, and to whom they reported daily. Every foreigner, even though he were known to be merely a traveler for pleasure, was watched, and everything that he did was carefully recorded. An inquiry addressed to the minister of police could bring from him at once complete particulars concerning almost any man or woman—where they had been at a given time, who were their friends, how they amused themselves, and a great deal more besides. All this information might not be used, and much of it was never used, yet scarcely anything was unknown to the men who cast this great spider's web over France, and who could from their files produce facts which, if generally known, would have wrecked families, destroyed reputations, and laid bare the dark secrets of many a life that seemed wholly spotless.

Gaboriau became fascinated by the thoroughness and precision of this remarkable system. He studied it in all its phases, and with the greatest care. As a result of this study, he wrote the novels which, with all their blemishes, are still read eagerly in many countries and in many languages.

Of these novels, the one best constructed and most deserving of fame is that entitled *M. Lecoq*, which he published in 1869, not many years before his death. In it is seen an ingenuity equal to that of Poe, while there is also shown a fair success in sketching character. Moreover, the author has introduced a new type of deductive reasoner which suggested to Conan Doyle the interesting Mycroft Holmes, brother of Sherlock Holmes, and that great detective's superior in the subtlety of his intellectual processes.

It will be remembered that the story of *M. Lecoq* opens with the commission of a crime, which, on the face of it, was not mysterious, but was apparently just one of those everyday tragedies that take place in the lowest quarters of Paris. Several detectives are making their rounds in the outskirts of the city, on a winter night, when they hear cries and pistol-shots from a low drinking-den of evil repute, situated in an open field on which the snow lies deep. The detectives hurry to the scene, surround the house, break in the door, and see, by the light of some flaming pine knots upon the hearth, that an act of violence has been committed. Tables and chairs have been overturned. Two men are stretched dead, while a third is already in the throes of death. Behind an oaken table stands a young and stalwart man, clenching a revolver. His torn garments resemble those of a railway porter. He declares that he has shot the men in self-defense, because they made a desperate attack upon him, believing him to be a police spy.

On the face of it there is nothing improbable in this. His story is believed by the men who arrest him, and especially by Gevrol, a police officer of some rank. The youngest of the detectives, however, whose name is Lecoq, feels a vague suspicion that the prisoner is not what he declares himself to be, and that underneath this crime there is hidden a tale of peculiar mystery. Two women are known to have been present, but they have escaped. There are also, to the mind of Lecoq, indications that the prisoner, in spite of his common clothing, is no common person; that he is a man of education, of great natural ability, and perhaps a rank; and finally that he had a male accomplice. These deductions of Lecoq are scouted by Gevrol; but nevertheless the young detective resolves to establish his theory and to solve the problem. From that moment there begins a conflict of wits between the prisoner on the one side and Lecoq on the other, the latter having the sympathy and confidence of the examining magistrate. The scene of the prisoner's examination by this magistrate is one of thrilling interest, and it gives to us Anglo-Saxons a vivid picture of the workings of French law in its assumptions that a prisoner is guilty unless he proves his innocence. The long, searching inquiry in which the judge alternately pleads with the accused and browbeats, threatens, and tortures him, hoping at last to break him down and wring from him a full confession, is wonderfully written.

The prisoner tells the magistrate a perfectly straightforward story, and yet there are parts of it which, under a keen cross-examination, show weakness and self-contradiction sufficient to strengthen the suspicion of Lecoq. Nevertheless, the detective is for the time quite baffled. All the external evidence that can be found curiously confirms the prisoner's story. Lecoq becomes convinced that there is a shrewd accomplice acting from without, who, in some mysterious way, is working as the prisoner's second self. The accused is kept in prison. His every action is watched, both night and day. Extraordinary tricks are devised to compel him to betray himself. They completely fail.

At last, Lecoq arranges matters so that the mysterious criminal may escape. Lecoq's plan is to follow him after he has escaped, and thus discover who are his friends and who he really is. The escape takes place. The prisoner threads his way through the most intricate mazes of criminal Paris, followed by Lecoq, who carries out the pursuit with the keenness of a hound; but at the end of the long hunt the object of it completely disappears over a high wall, which surrounds the magnificent grounds and mansion of the Duc de Sairmeuse, one of the noblest members of the French aristocracy. Though Lecoq and the police at once enter the mansion, and search all the rooms in it, their bird apparently has flown. A ball and reception are in progress at the great house. There are no traces in it of the fleeing criminal; and Lecoq for the time confesses himself defeated, suffering in silence the jeers of his associates, and especially of Gevrol, who has become jealous of his able and enthusiastic subordinate.

Lecoq finally betakes himself to the house of an old retired tradesman, who is an amateur in criminology and detection. This person, named Tabaret, but known to the police as Pere Tirauclair, is much of the time confined in bed by gout. For his own amusement, however, he collects all the details of every conspicuous crime and studies them with intense avidity, not as crimes, but as psychological problems. Given all the facts, he can, by the unerring process of pure reason, sift out the false from the true, the irrelevant from the essential, and go swiftly to the heart of any mystery. It is he who gives Lecoq the clue to the identity of the escaped prisoner.

Here is the original suggestion of Mycroft Holmes, who, it will be remembered, was fat and lazy, spending his spare hours in the Diogenes Club, of which no member ever spoke to any other member. Mycroft Holmes does not trouble himself with active work. He relies entirely upon his deductive powers and relentless logic. It may be said that this is only a copy of Poe's Auguste Dupin, but such is not the case. Dupin did "outside work," personally visited the scenes of crimes, inserted advertisements in newspapers, and, in fact, employed the whole machinery of detection. But Mycroft Holmes, like old Pere Tirauclair, simply thought out the problem presented to him, and then directed others what to do. Here we find a conception more attractive even than that of Poe; and the literary touches of Gaboriau and Doyle give us a genuine personality that far surpasses the interest of a mere calculating machine.

It is true that Gaboriau mars his story by injecting into it a long secondary narrative. Conan Doyle made precisely the same mistake in his first successful detective tale, "A Study in Scarlet"; but it was a mistake which was never repeated. Gaboriau, therefore, is a link between Edgar Allan Poe and Conan Doyle, just as Poe himself is a link between Voltaire and Gaboriau.

Conan Doyle is the supreme writer of detective stories. He, like Gaboriau, plays the game fairly, since he lets the reader have all the knowledge which Holmes himself possesses. It has been written of his tales:

> The really remarkable thing about these stories is that, before the mystery is solved, the reader is put in possession of every fact material to its solution. The puzzle is handed over with no missing pieces. We are freely offered every single bit of evidence which could convince the detective. That is, the reader has been kept in exactly the mental state of the ingenuous Dr. Watson, or the blundering official, Gregson. He has seen all there is to be seen; and if he fails to interpret events aright, it is simply because his own acuteness does not equal that of the detective.

In other words, the cleverness of Doyle lies in his simplicity and frankness, and also in the fact that his people are living, breathing, human beings. One grows fond of Sherlock Holmes, not only because of his wonderful mind, but because of his faults and failings. His addiction to the cocaine habit, his dislike of women, his skill as a boxer, his need when thinking out a problem of smoking great quantities of shag tobacco which he keeps in an old slipper, his trick of shooting bullets into his mantelpiece so as to form the royal initials (V. R.), the general disorderliness of his housekeeping—all these things give him individuality. We feel that we actually know him. We are almost as much interested in his personal whims and prejudices, and in his casual talks with Watson, as we are with his triumphs of detection.

And the same interest adheres to Watson, that admirable, commonplace, and usual Briton, and in a less degree to the official police who employ Sherlock's skill and then take credit to themselves. No imitators of Poe, or of Doyle himself, have been successful in this thing. They can think out problems, but they cannot create men and women. Compare, for instance, the detective stories lately written by Jacques Futrelle and M. Gaston Leroux. Their work is purely machine work. To go further back, even Balzac, who made an attempt at detective fiction in his *Ferragus*, was wise enough to see that this was not his forte. He and Ponson du Terrail in this one particular field seem stodgy and mechanical. Yet even Gaboriau is superior to Poe. Had there been no Gaboriau, we might never have had that fascinating cycle of stories which Conan Doyle has written around the great detective who lived in Baker Street, and whose name is as well known all over the world today as that of Shylock, Falstaff, or any other creation of Shakespeare himself, with, perhaps, Hamlet as the one exception.

Of course, this seems extravagant; but the contemporary public is seldom a good judge of what is best or of what is worst in the writers of their own time. They either overpraise or underestimate. It is, or ought to be, a truism that professional critics of literature are generally the very last persons in the world to recognize the value of new literature when they see it. This is partly because such standards as they have are purely conventional, and partly because they themselves are timorous and mistrustful and afraid of making mistakes.

Hence they hesitate to commit themselves to a definite opinion until they are pretty sure that they are on the side of the majority. The result is that they follow where they ought to lead, and are apt to come in at the tail of the procession when they ought to come in at its head. Just as the venerable Austrian commanders in Italy were convinced that Napoleon knew nothing about the art of war because he was defeating them in reckless defiance of the rules laid down in the military text-books, so our literary critics would not admit that Kipling's first five books had any value; for these were brilliant in an utterly new way, and not in the thoroughly recognized old way. Originality is terribly disconcerting to unoriginal people. They think it frivolous or "unsound" or "odd." They never quite approve of it. Therefore, they glorify Robert Louis Stevenson for those productions of his that are good in a conventional style, but ignore his extraordinary tour de force which is unique in literature. For, a century hence, *Treasure Island* and *The Master of Ballantrae* and all the essays will be only names to the reading public, while *Dr. Jekyll and Mr. Hyde* will stand as the most striking allegory ever written on the curious duality of man's moral nature.

The case of Arthur Conan Doyle is almost as interesting as the case of Kipling, in kind though not in degree. Doyle does not take himself and his writings very seriously. Neither did Plautus or Shakespeare, for that matter. Most of his books are admirable examples of the story-telling quality which in some mysterious fashion makes its possessor able to give real interest to even a commonplace narrative. In fact, the least important of his stories—as for instance some of those in *Round the Red Lamp*—are worth reading many times. They may be as improbable as the one about the resuscitated Egyptian mummy or the electrocution at Los Amigos; but all the same you will be glad to know them and you will wish for more. In his historical novels, *The White Company* and *Micah Clark*, this story-telling is of a high order, yet still not going beyond the limits of great cleverness. The critics, however, would select these books as containing the best of which Doyle is capable. The one thing of his that is really indicative of creative genius they merely smile upon indulgently, and pass by with as little notice as they would give to a dime-novel. It never occurs to them that English fiction was permanently enriched when Doyle began the cycle of stories whose protagonist is Sherlock Holmes.

It is likely that most literary critics, if asked to give an opinion about these remarkable stories, would at once compare them with those of Gaboriau and feel that there was nothing more to say. But, as a matter of fact, the Sherlock Holmes stories are not only immensely superior to anything of Gaboriau's, but in some respects the best of them are better than those tales of Poe which treat of crime and its detection. Gaboriau is an excellent literary artisan. His mysteries are very neatly constructed. The parts all dovetail perfectly. But they have little artistic value, and the unraveling of their complicated plots is like the dissection of a puzzle which interests by its ingenuity, but appeals neither to the intellect nor to the imagination. Poe, on the other hand, is highly intellectual, and in "The Murders in the Rue Morgue," for instance, he stirs the imagination very powerfully. He can rouse the sense of horror and make his mystery deepen into ghastliness and terror.

Conan Doyle, however, can do these things and give us still another ingredient—the human element. Sherlock Holmes, as has been said, would interest us simply as a man. His curiously varied tastes, his fondness for good music and rare books, his disorderly rooms, his utter boredom when absorbed in disentangling mysteries, his prodigious consumption of shag tobacco when working out his problems, his addiction to the cocaine habit—a curious touch—all these things amuse or interest or pique us until we grow fond of him and get at last to know him almost as well as though we, too, shared his rooms in Baker Street. Watson is another creation. Like all true artists, who do their best work by instinct rather than self-consciously, it is probable that Doyle had no idea of how supremely clever a thing it was to make Watson a companion and chronicler and also the foil of Sherlock Holmes. Watson, the matter-of-fact, sensible, and friendly surgeon, always planting both his broad feet squarely on the earth, has a lack of insight that makes Holmes' wonderful intuition appear twice as wonderful by the force of contrast. Moreover, by letting Watson be the narrator of the stories, they are made to seem always plausible to the reader, because of their sober, unemotional manner. Gregson, of the regular detective force, is also a type drawn adequately with a few broad strokes. Beside them Gaboriau's Gevrol is shadowy and unreal. The creation of Mycroft Holmes was a stroke of genius. That Sherlock Holmes should have had a brother, superior in inductive reasoning even to Sherlock himself, is interesting; that he should be fat and luxurious and far too lazy to use his gifts in any practical way, is delicious. The likeness of mind and the utter unlikeness of temperament between the indolent Mycroft and the keen, nervous, high-strung Sherlock is fascinating. That Mycroft Holmes is introduced in but a single story—that of the Greek interpreter—shows a remarkable artistic self-control on the part of Doyle. The glimpse that is given of him is tantalizing. One longs to know more about him, but his creator very wisely stayed his hand.

The very best of all these stories are not the long ones—"A Study in Scarlet" and "The Sign of the Four"—though each of these contains many very striking things, and the first of them (of which Doyle himself is said to have thought so little that he sold the manuscript outright for $125) introduces us to Sherlock at the outset of his career. There is no doubt that the most finished and most effective tale is that of "The Speckled Band." This is a marvel of construction and of execution not merely worthy of Poe, but better than Poe's best. From the very first page the reader's interest is riveted upon a mystery which, as it develops, is utterly inscrutable and fascinates one by its undefined yet very evident horror. The inexplicable death of the elder sister, the warnings given to the surviving girl, the peculiar whistle in the night, the clanging sound of metal, the strange discoveries made by Holmes, and then that nerve-racking vigil in the blackness of midnight with the hideous revelation at the end of it—I know of nothing in fiction of this genre which possesses an interest so absorbingly intense.

Of a different character is "The Naval Treaty," which I place next to "The Speckled Band" in merit as a story. This tale affords a good example of the method by which the circumstances of a mysterious event are set forth quite frankly and yet in such a way that the perfectly simple and obvious explanation never once occurs to you. The draft of a secret naval treaty between England and Italy is to be copied by young Phelps, of the British Foreign Office, who is a near relative of Lord Holdhurst, the Foreign Minister. No one but Phelps and Lord Holdhurst know of it. The reputation of both these men is at stake, if the terms of the treaty shall be discovered; and, moreover, serious diplomatic complications will ensue. Phelps has remained at his desk in the Foreign Office after everyone but the janitor has left, and then he begins to make the required draft. Finding that it will keep him later than he had expected, he goes downstairs to ask the doorkeeper to get him a cup of coffee. While he is giving the order, he hears a bell in his room ring, and, rushing back again, he finds the room empty and the treaty gone. Now, in the first place, as no human being knew that the treaty was there, and, in the second place, as the thief, instead of stealing it and sneaking quietly away, rang the bell to announce his presence, the problem seems on the face of it insoluble; yet the explanation of it, when it comes, is really the simplest and most natural thing in the world. Herein Doyle's plots differ utterly from Gaboriau's. Those of the French writer are complex to a degree; those of Doyle are simplicity itself. The reader is just as hopelessly puzzled by them, but the solution, when it comes, comes not as a mathematical demonstration, but as a flash of light in a dark place—illuminating, surprising, delighting, all at once.

After the two stories just mentioned, I should place, without attempting to assign them a definite order of merit, "Silver Blaze," "The Resident Patient," "The Engineer's Thumb," "The Boscombe Valley Mystery," "The Five Orange

Pips," "The Reigate Puzzle," and "The Final Problem." Three stories make too strong a demand upon the reader's credulity. These are "The Red Headed League," "A Case of Identity," and "The Man with the Twisted Lip," yet the first of them is none the less one of the most absorbing interest. There is, indeed, not one story in the whole cycle which does not contain many touches that positively fascinate one by their ingenuity and unexpectedness.

Doyle will sooner or later get the recognition from the critics which he has already won from the reading public. His hold upon that public is an extraordinary one. Many books of the day sell by hundreds of thousands, yet they are not talked about and no one clamors for more from their author's pens. But in the case of the Sherlock Holmes adventures, the public not only buys and reads, but discusses them continually; and it has so strenuously insisted upon having more that Doyle has been obliged to yield to the demand. This compliance has been most unfortunate for the author's reputation. He has written not because he wished to write, but because he was made to do so. Hence, the later stories about Sherlock Holmes are feeble trash with the exception of *The Hound of the Baskervilles*. Whatever is best in his studies of the great detective will be found in the *Adventures* and the *Memoirs*. The others will be forgotten, just as *Dred* has been forgotten, while *Uncle Tom's Cabin* is sure of immortality. But when the dross shall have been purged away, there will remain a group of stories so fascinating as to give their author the highest rank among those who have attempted this very interesting kind of fiction.

On O. Henry

Frederic Taber Cooper

This biographical and critical consideration of O. Henry and his work at once questions the immense popularity of his stories and praises where the critic believes praise is due. Cooper, for example, sees none of the excellent local color so often touted as a primary reason for these stories' great appeal—for him, O. Henry's local color amounts to no more than "a few names of streets and buildings, printed with capital letters." He does, however, recognize the "economy of means, that unerring instinct for ending a story" that showcase O. Henry's technical abilities. This approach allows Cooper to avoid the pitfalls of other critics, professional and otherwise, who were too quick either to declare O. Henry the most clever writer of short prose literary history had ever seen, or to dismiss him as a gimmicky flash in the pan whose stories pander to the broadest denominators of public taste. Purveyor of pulp or literary artisan? Narrative genius or formulaic hack? Operating between the crude biases of these extremes, Cooper offers a valuable consideration of O. Henry's place in American letters.

It is a sufficiently common figure of speech to characterize the careers of certain persons as meteoric—but usually with no conception of the length of time that it may have taken the meteor to gain the requisite velocity and momentum to produce its brief, fiery burst, and no thought of the stray fragments that remain after the burst is over to awaken the curious appreciation of the enlightened few. If we accept this broader view, then O. Henry was quite literally a literary meteor. Although he had served an apprenticeship of a score of years, he remained, up to within half a decade of his death, practically unknown to the general reading public; and by then, in half a decade more, he will already have begun to be forgotten. Yet for just a few intervening years he achieved a popularity unparalleled in its swift development and its extent by any modern American writer of short stories. And not least surprising was the variety of taste to which he appealed, the range in education, culture and social class of his reading public. Considered as an article of merchandise, his stories have commanded a market rate rivaled only by Kipling; considered as literature, they have formed the theme of more than one grave and reverent professor of English Letters. The meteor has blazed, and burst, and burned itself out; and the interesting question not unnaturally arises, to what extent was O. Henry's vogue justified? Is the popular verdict greatly in error? Does his fame of the passing hour rest upon a solid foundation?

One takes up the answer with a certain amount of diffidence. As was said in another critical article in one of the magazines quite recently, but while the author of *Cabbages and Kings* was still with us, such matters "rest upon the knees of the Gods." It is always easier to dogmatize as to what posterity ought to do than to predict what that profoundly unknown quantity really will do. Nevertheless, certain opinions may be ventured with some assurance, provided we base them first, upon a few established facts regarding the personal O. Henry—his life, his temperament, his attitude toward his craft, and secondly, upon the really salient points of his own productions.

In the first place, then, at the risk of tediously repeating what has recently become a commonplace of the daily press, let us summarize the main facts in the life of this particular American story teller. That his real name was Sidney Porter and that he happened to be born in Greensborough, North Carolina, in the year 1867, is not material; but it helps to complete the record. The fact that his health, as a boy, was rather poor and that consequently he was sent to a Texas ranch at a time when otherwise he would have gone to college, has a more direct bearing upon our problem. He was not of the stuff from which ranchmen and cowboys are made; and, although with characteristic facility he picked up his surprising amount of the picturesque idiom of the ranch, a scant three years had satiated him with the life. All this time, somewhere in the back of his mind had lurked persistently the ambition to write. Perhaps one of the most curious facts in the world of letters is the unlikely sources from which the public favorites among writers spring. When one sees the apparent hopelessness of conditions that have given birth to some of the successful fiction makers of today, even the most self-confident critics hesitate to say to an apparently hopeless novice: Give it up; there is no chance for you.

The life of the ranch had re-established Porter's health. Following the insistent call of letters, he went to Houston and secured a position on a daily paper, *The Post*. It is curious how biographers insist upon mixing up essentials and non-essentials. Much has been made of the fact that *The Houston Post* paid Porter fifteen dollars a week and that the editor assured him that within five years he would be earning a hundred a week on a New York newspaper. So far as this means anything, it means that Porter must have been more successful as a reporter than the editor was as a prophet. Many more than five years passed before he reached New York. The essential facts, so far, are that he had an inborn desire to write, a frail constitution which debarred him from a college education and the good luck to strike almost simultaneously a healthful climate and a newspaper opening. The following items have their importance: after a year on *The Post*, he went to Austin and purchased for the sum of two hundred and fifty dollars a newspaper named *The Iconoclast* from its owner, a certain Brann. The latter, having withdrawn to Waco, and perhaps regretting his bargain, asked Porter to give him back the paper's name. Our author, with characteristic generosity, consented and rechristened his own paper *The Rolling Stone*. Whatever symbolism there may be in names, this particular paper promptly rolled itself out of existence, and the future O. Henry went into voluntary exile in Central America. The fact that he went there with a friend who "intended to go into the fruit business, but didn't," is evidence of a credulity characteristic of him, not only then but later—as subsequent anecdotes show.

What he did and what he saw in Central America, one gleans between the lines of *Cabbages and Kings*, but the one authentic bit of autobiography of that period is the single laconic sentence: "Most of the time I knocked around with the refugees and consuls." Porter's subsequent movements are given still more briefly in the few meager printed accounts. He returned to Texas, then removed to New Orleans, "where he began more consistently to work as a writer," and in 1902 came to New York, having received from *Ainslee's Magazine* the offer of one hundred dollars each for a dozen stories. From that time, until his death, Porter made New York his home, exhibiting that extreme, almost exaggerated affection for the metropolis that is peculiar to the Manhattanite by adoption.

Now, the years about which we know least are probably the important ones, the years of growth and slow accretion. The record, as it stands, fails to explain. It shows a man of naturally roving spirit, whose schoolbook has been experience, hard and practical, and who toiled for twenty years before beginning to reap his reward. It is easy enough to write sagely that "his wanderings have influenced his work," that "Texas gives the setting of short stories called *The Heart of the West*," that "Central America is the scene of *Cabbages and Kings*," and that New York gives the background for *The Four Million*, *The Voice of the City* and *The Trimmed Lamp*. This all sounds as though it meant something; but in reality it does not. There are probably many thousands of people whose lot in life has taken them successively to Texas, to Central America and to New York, yet there is only one O. Henry. What would really be worth knowing is what he was thinking about, through all these formative years; what books he read, and which especially impressed him; what sort of work, in kind and quality, he did on the various newspapers with which he connected himself; and above all, where he learned his technique of the short story, and what models, if any, he consciously imitated. Of all this we have only a few meager and tantalizing glimpses, like the following paragraph, published in a comparatively recent interview:

> I did more reading between my thirteenth and nineteenth years than I have done in all the years that have passed since then. And my taste at that time was much better than it is today; for I used to read nothing but the classics. Burton's *Anatomy of Melancholy* and Lane's translation of the *Arabian Nights* were my favorites.

The *Anatomy of Melancholy* and the *Arabian Nights* are indisputably classics, but there is nothing in either that could have given a hint of that nice economy of means, that unerring instinct for ending a story at just the right instant, and with just the right phrase, that makes so many of O. Henry's stories models of technical skill. Because of this constructive gift, he has not infrequently been hailed as the "Yankee Maupassant," and yet those who knew him best give assurance that O. Henry either never made the acquaintance of the author of "La Parure," or else read him only after the great bulk of his own writings was completed. And it is equally doubtful whether he became acquainted with French technique through what is probably the next best medium—the short stories of H. C. Bunner. Apparently the O. Henry story is to a large extent an independent development, born of an instinct for getting the sharpest possible narrative effects.

Now, it is idle to deny many of O. Henry's very genuine merits. He was technically a master of his craft, even though to the practiced eye certain tricks of his trade stick out somewhat conspicuously. He had mingled on terms of frank comradeship with all sorts and conditions of men, the tramp, the clerk, the ward politician, the city policeman, the shop and factory girl, the human derelict at home and abroad; and he has a faculty compared by more than once critic to that of Dickens, for catching both the humor and the pathos of these alien lives. Francis Hackett, writing recently in the *Chicago Evening Post*, made the following comment:

> To O. Henry, the clerk is neither abnormal or subnormal; he is simply $15-a-week humanity. He has specialized in this humanity with loving care, with a Kiplingesque attention to detail. But his is far from the humorless method of Gissing and Merrick, who were no more happy in a boarding-house than Thoreau would have been in the Waldorf-Astoria.

One is tempted to ask parenthetically why, in the name of all that makes good art, an author should be required to be happy in a boarding-house, or a corner grocery, or an East Side tenement, in order to write of them truly and with understanding. The important fact is not whether O. Henry was happy in the company of clerks, but whether he understood them—and of this his stories leave not the shadow of a doubt. It is true, however, that O. Henry's likes and dislikes do occasionally intrude themselves between the story and the reader—and to the lover of a finished art, this is not a merit, but quite distinctly a fly in the ointment of our enjoyment.

Another quality for which O. Henry has been overpraised by nearly every writer who has attempted a critical analysis of his work, is the excellence of his local descriptions, the accuracy with which he makes you feel that a certain story not only happened in New York, but that it was part and parcel of the city itself, and of no other place in the world. It is extremely enlightening, as regards O. Henry's attitude toward fiction in general and towards his own work in particular, to read the following frank confession:

People say I know New York well! But change Twenty-third Street in one of my New York stories to Main Street, rub out the Flatiron Building and put in the Town Hall. Then the story will fit just as truly elsewhere. At least I hope this is the case with what I write. So long as your story is true to life, the mere change of local color will set it in the East, West, South or North. The characters in the *Arabian Nights* parade up and down Broadway at midday, or Main Street in Dallas, Texas.

When I recently ran across this paragraph for the first time, it gave me a rather keen delight; because, personally, I never could see the excellence of O. Henry's local color; I never could feel that a few names of streets and buildings, printed with capital letters, seemed to give the illusion of that indefinable atmosphere which a person born and bred into a certain city absorbs from a thousand subtle little sights and sounds and smells, such as that city and none other has to offer. It is a comfort to discover, not merely that the fault was not a lack of perception on my part, but a deliberate choice upon the part of O. Henry—in short, that he not only neglected an essential article in Maupassant's declaration of faith as an artist, but that he openly avowed his disbelief in it. It would be interesting to know what he would have thought of Flaubert's insistence upon the supreme necessity, if you are describing only a tree, a horse or a dog, of catching its special physiognomy so unerringly that it could not be confused with any other tree, horse or dog in the whole world.

Yet it is easy to understand O. Henry's vogue; he appealed to a wide range of men and women, because he wrote of a wide range with sympathy and understanding. He appealed to the wide class that is repelled by anything like academic nicety of speech, by the raciness of his phrase and vocabulary, his habit of making the English language a servant rather than a master. Much of his humor lies in his verbal audacities—and for that very reason his is doomed within a decade to seem in a measure already out of date. And his habit of invoking local and temporal allusions, not merely as subordinate details, but at times as the turning-point of a story, is another factor that will hasten the wane of his popularity. Take, for example, one of the best stories that he ever wrote, "The Rose of Dixie." It is a story of an old Southern colonel, who has undertaken to edit a magazine exclusively in the interests of the "fair daughters and brave sons" of Dixieland. Handicapped by the Colonel's strong sectional prejudices, the magazine is not a financial success; so the stockholders suggest that the aid of a certain Thacker, famed for successes in forcing up the circulation of lagging periodicals, shall be invoked. The Colonel rejects Thacker's much too radical suggestions, but at the same time hints mysteriously at an important article that he has on hand, an article brimful of wise philosophy of life—but unfortunately written by one regarding whose qualifications he has not yet sufficiently informed himself. The tale, in order to be appreciated, has to be read. No amount of skill in epitomizing can begin to convey the humor of the denouement, when the article at last appears with the title emblazoned with local significance, in prominent full-faced type, and the name of the author so minute as to be almost illegible, below it—and that, too, the name of one who, as the time the "Rose of Dixie" was written, happened to be Chief Executive of the nation. A generation hence, the edge of the joke will be quite gone; indeed, it is already somewhat dulled.

One disadvantage under which a writer of short stories labors is that it is out of the question to analyze at any length even a tithe of this writings. Thus, in the case of O. Henry, one would be glad to dwell at some length upon each separate volume, to analyze the clever mechanism of *Cabbages and Kings*, whereby the reader is carried through a lengthy string of apparently slightly correlated tales, and does not suspect, until the final page is turned, that underlying them all is a mystery, a series of cross-purposes, straightened out only when the bits of human flotsam finally meet and exchange confidences on a North River pier in New York. But to stop long over any one volume, or even over a considerable number of stories, would serve no special purpose. The more you read them, the more you realize that there is a certain sameness about his themes and his structure, that he has just a few formulas that he invokes over and over again. There is, for instance, the formula of cross-purposes, like the story, if memory is not at fault in details, of the man who pawned his watch, to buy his wife for Christmas a fur neck-piece to match her muff—unaware that she in turn had sacrificed her muff, in order to buy him a watch-fob. Or again, there is the irony-of-fate formula, as exemplified in the story of "Soapy and the Anthem," in which a tramp, having made up his mind that a few months on the Island will be the pleasantest arrangement that he can make for winter, proceeds to attempt to get himself arrested, by swindling a restaurant keeper out of a meal, by breaking a window, by insulting a woman, and all to no purpose; fate under one guise or another, intervenes to defeat his plans. And then, at last, he is passing a church door, and hears the swelling notes of a fine old anthem, some softening memory of childhood steals over him, and he finds himself, unkempt and ragged as he is, drawn irresistibly into the church, with a growing resolution to turn over a new leaf—a policeman, deciding that he is lurking there for no good purpose, runs him in, and Soapy, now that he no longer wishes it, finds himself on his way to the Island.

And then again, there is what we may call the "inertia of human nature" formula—the type of story based upon a subtle appreciation of the fact that people often think that they have learned a lesson, but, as soon as the stress is over, drop back again into their old rut. One of the best of this class is a story in the volume called *The Trimmed Lamp*. It is not necessarily the best of the collection, but somehow it made a rather special appeal to the present writer, and seems worth giving in some detail.

It is merely the story of a commonplace man married to a commonplace wife and living in a commonplace little apartment on a salary the smallness of which also seems to have the element of commonplaceness. A story, you will perceive, in which the temperamental barometer on the whole stands rather low. After the glamor of the honeymoon wore off, the man fell gradually into the habit of spending his evenings away from the home atmosphere. As surely as the hands of the clock came around to half-past eight he would reach for his hat. "Now, where are you going, I should like to know?" the wife's querulous voice would question, and his stereotyped answer would be flung back through the closing door, "Just going down to play pool with the boys for half an hour." But one night when he comes home there is no wife to meet him, no dinner waiting, nothing but a pervading disorder and a hasty note telling him that she has been called away by the sudden news of her mother's serious illness. Disconsolately he makes a comfortless meal from cold remnants found in the icebox, the loneliness of the apartment each instant forcing itself into his consciousness. It is the first night since their marriage that she has been away from him, the first time that he has asked himself what life would be without her. He begins to regret the hours of her society he has voluntarily lost, the evenings he has gone out and left her to bear the same solitude from which he is now suffering. Never again, he tells himself, never again! He will make it up to his wife when she comes back, he will take her out more, to theaters and all that sort of thing; she shall never again be left to the ghastly loneliness of these silent rooms. And, in the midst of his good resolutions, the door opens and the wife walks in; mother's illness was a false alarm, she did not need to stay, after all. This topic occupies them until she finishes dinner. Then, as the hands of the clock move around to half-past eight, the man reaches mechanically for his hat. "Now where are you going, I should like to know?" comes the stereotyped question, with all its wonted querulousness; and the stereotyped answer comes back through the closing door, "Just going down to play pool with the boys for half an hour."

Yet, in the case of O. Henry, more perhaps than in that of any other popular story writer of his generation, the relative merits and deficiencies of his stories are a matter of individual opinion. Discuss Kipling in any group of average well-read men and women, and you will find a certain amount of disagreement; some will hold that the earlier tales are easily superior to the later, and others will insist on the opposite view; some will maintain that "They" is his most finished masterpiece, the one story that stands alone upon a lofty height, and others will see little or nothing in it. But on the whole, the world agrees pretty well in singling out "Without Benefit of Clergy," "The Drums of the Fore-and-Aft," "The Man Who Would Be King," "On the City Wall," "The Courtship of Dinah Shadd," while "An Habitation Enforced," "Mrs. Bathurst," and "A Deal in Cotton" would come in as pretty close seconds. But if you try the same experiment regarding O. Henry's stories, you will find a very different state of matters. Almost everyone present will have read him, and almost everyone will have his or her own personal preference, backed up by reasons to justify it. Half of the time they will not remember the title—in spite of the pains that Porter is said to have taken over his titles, they are not of the kind that stick in the memory—sometimes a good many of the details will have faded out; but what people remember is the sharp, unlooked-for twist at the end of the story, like the snap of a whip in a practiced hand. Do you remember, someone is sure to ask, that story of the local champion prize-fighter, who is just starting in on his honeymoon, and whose bride expresses a wish for peaches? It is late at night; and even in New York, even in the ward where he is something of a power, peaches in the off-season are not easy to find. Everywhere he is offered oranges, big, thin-skinned, juicy oranges—but not a peach is to be found. At last he remembers a certain high life gambling resort, where everything is done in lavish style, and where the buffet is never lacking in luscious hothouse fruits. Now in all his devious career, he has stuck to his standards of loyalty, he has stood for a "square deal" among his kind. But tonight he is in a dilemma; his bride has demanded peaches, and peaches she must have, loyalty or no loyalty. Accordingly, he goes contrary to the ethics of his class, takes part in a police raid on the gambling house, and in the midst of a general rough-and-tumble fight, which is a gem of its kind, manages to make his escape with two rather dilapidated peaches. And now comes the snap of the whip; when he hands them to his expectant bride, she looks at them disappointedly, and says, "Oh, did I say peaches? It was oranges that I wanted!"

"You haven't told that quite right!" someone else rejoins, "you don't emphasize the oranges enough. Don't you remember that everywhere he goes they say to him, 'Now, if it was only oranges you wanted!' and at the last place, he turns on them savagely and interrupts with: 'If anyone dares to say oranges again to me, I'll—' and words fail him! But I'll tell you a story ever so much better than that, and that's the 'Jimmy Valentine' one. There's a short story that really has some substance to it, a short story that had in it the material of a full-length play. Supposing you should give a story writer the following problem: Let the hero be a criminal, perhaps an escaped convict; under another name, he has found honest employment in a town where his past is not known; he has won the respect of his new friends, and the love of a good woman; his future seems assured. And suddenly, as he is in the act of destroying the only remaining evidences of the past, of cutting himself off even from the memory of his old life, fate brings him face to face with an extraordinary dilemma; someone very close to the woman he loves is in danger of death, tragic and agonizing; and it is only by revealing his crime-stained past, only by resorting to his criminal skill that he can save her. In other words, it is the man's reformation, his newly acquired tenderness of heart that is his undoing; there is the problem—and if you assigned it to a score of writers, I doubt if any one of them would have got a quarter of the possibilities out of it that O. Henry did."

"That is all very well," objects someone else at this point, "'Jimmy Valentine' was a good job of its kind. But he deliberately spoiled it at the end by one sentimental touch, the popular happy ending. We all know that in real life the detective who had spent weary months in tracking down an escaped convict would not let him go at last, with the tools of his trade in his hands, just because he 'cracked' a safe in time to save a child from smothering! But if you want O. Henry at his best, take a story like the one about the little girl whose mother 'didn't like that she should play in the street,' and whose father, red-headed and sullen-tempered, spent his Sunday afternoons sitting by the window, in his shirt-sleeves and with his heels on the ledge, leisurely emptying a tin can of beer. 'Papa, won't you play checkers with me?' the little girl asks wistfully. 'No, I'm busy; run along and play in the street,' growls the man, and the little girl goes, in spite of the mother's feeble protest, 'I don't like that she should play in the street.' Well, when we see that child again, a few years have passed; the street has done its worst for her, and she is in cruel trouble. The man whom she has loved too rashly openly favors another girl at a big East Side dance hall, when, true to her street training, she draws a knife, stabs her rival, and ends her misery in the East River. The scene shifts from this world to the next; an angel of the heavenly detective corps has brought up for judgment the bedraggled soul of a poor drowned girl, and is proceeding to press the charge. 'Hold on!' says St. Peter—or words to that effect, 'You have arrested the wrong person. The one you want to look for is a red-headed man, in his shirt-sleeves, drinking beer on Sunday out of a tin can. You'll lose your job if you aren't more careful; that's the fourth mistake you've made this week!'"

There, in brief, we have a fairly wide and representative selection of O. Henry's stories. They do not pretend to include even a tithe of those one would like to mention, if space allowed; yet such as are here included show him pretty nearly at his best, wisely comprehensive of human foibles, indulgently ironic, yet with an underlying touch of sympathy that illumines and softens much that is sordid and commonplace. That he was a genuine artist cannot be questioned; that he was overrated by his own people and generation is more than possible. That the large element of what was local and temporal is likely to prove a heavy handicap in the race for immortality cannot be denied. As Anatole France sagely remarked, "one must be light, in order to fly across the ages." At all events, frankness demands recognition of the fact that O. Henry, while not limited to a narrow range, was not possessed of a conspicuously wide one; that he had already achieved enough on which to rest a substantial fame, and that it is doubtful whether, had he lived, he would ever have surpassed what he has already done. His early death has robbed us of the man, but in all likelihood it did not seriously rob him of any laurels.

On Ambrose Bierce

Frederic Taber Cooper

Cooper's critical treatment of Ambrose Bierce—composed shortly after the publication of a multi-volume collection of Bierce's complete works—is alternately grudgingly tolerant and full of praise. He is merely—sometimes barely—tolerant of Bierce's own critical judgments, believing that Bierce has taken "upon himself the task of reprimanding the universe," of destroying the conventional, accepted mode of criticism but suggesting nothing new or better to take it's place. Cooper is careful to point out, however, that the "value of Bierce as a critic lies solely in his fearlessness and downright sincerity." Regarding Bierce's fictional writing, notice Cooper's discussion of what Bierce calls the "basic quality in all art," which is unity in narrative elements, or "totality of effect." Cooper's criticism of Bierce's ideas on effect recalls W. C. Brownell's criticism of Edgar Allan Poe (see Brownell's essay on Poe, also in this volume), who had a similar focus and who suffered similar, and somewhat more brutal, critical attacks. Again, though, Cooper's remarks are qualified: while criticizing Bierce's allegiance to what he believes is a superficial narrative component, he at the same time praises Bierce's "wizardry of word and phrase, his almost magnetic power to make the absurd, the grotesque, the impossible, carry an overwhelming conviction." It is this balance that makes Cooper's essay most useful—it neither praises too thickly nor attacks too sharply. It offers an even account, pointing out weaknesses Bierce's readers may have not considered while acknowledging achievements they may have not yet had occasion to appreciate.

Regarding literary criticism, Bierce says quite frankly "the saddest thing about the trade of writing is that the writer can never know, nor hope to know, if he is a good workman. In literary criticism, there are no criteria, no accepted standards of excellence by which to test the work." Now there is just enough truth in this attitude of mind to make it a rather dangerous one. If there were literally no accepted standards in any of the arts, no principles to which a certain influential majority of critical minds had given their adhesion, then literature and all the arts would be in a state of perennial anarchy. But of course any writer who believes in his heart that there are no criteria will necessarily remain in lifelong ignorance regarding his own worth, for it is only through learning how to criticize others sanely and justly that one acquires even the rudiments of self-criticism. And incidentally, it may be observed that no better proof of Bierce's fundamental lack of this valuable asset could be asked than the retention in these ten volumes of a considerable amount of journalistic rubbish side by side with flashes of undoubted genius. Bierce's entire essay on the subject of criticism is a sort of literary agnosticism, a gloomy denial of faith. He has no confidence in the judgment of the general public nor in that of the professional critic. He admits that "in a few centuries, more or less, there may arrive a critic that we call Posterity"— but Posterity, he complains, is a trifle slow. Accordingly, since the worth of any contemporary writer is reduced to mere guess-work, he, Ambrose Bierce, has scant use for his contemporaries. He has very definite ideas regarding the training of young writers and tells us at some length the course through which he would like to put an imaginary pupil, but he adds:

If I caught him reading a newly published book, save by way of penance, it would go hard with him. Of our modern education he should have enough to read the ancients: Plato, Aristotle, Marcus Aurelius, Seneca, and that lot—custodians of most of what is worth knowing.

In spite of the pains to which Bierce goes to deny that he is a *laudator temporis acti*, the term fits him admirably—and nowhere is this attitude of mind more conspicuous than in his treatment of the modern novel. It is important, however, to get clearly in mind the arbitrary sense in which he uses the word novel as distinguished from what he calls romance. His occasional half-definitions are somewhat confusing; but apparently by the novel he means realistic fiction as distinguished from romantic fiction—a distinction complicated by the further idiosyncrasy that by realism he understands almost exclusively the commonplaces of actuality and by romanticism any happening which is out of the ordinary. The novel, then, in his sense of the word is "a snow plant; it has no root in the permanent soil of literature, and does not long to hold its place; it is of the lowest form of imagination." And again: "The novel bears the same relation to literature that the panorama bears to painting; with whatever skill and feeling the panorama is painted, it must lack that basic quality in all art, unity, or totality of effect." He seems utterly unaware that the great gain in modern fiction, the one indisputable factor that separates it from the fiction of half a century ago, is precisely the basic quality of unity. The modern novel whose technique most nearly approaches perfection is the one which when read rapidly with "a virgin attention at a single sitting"—to borrow Bierce's own phrase—gives an impression of as single-hearted a purpose as one finds in the most faultless of Maupassant's three-thousand word masterpieces. It is quite possible for any well-trained reader to go through even the longest of novels in a single sitting. The present writer would feel himself grievously at fault if he interrupted his first reading of any novel that had been given him for the purpose of a review; and he well remembers that in only two recent cases did he become conscious of the prolonged strain: namely, Kipling's *Kim*, which required an uninterrupted attention of eight and one-half hours, and *The Golden Bowl*, of James, which required somewhat more than eleven. Bierce's attitude, however, is partly explained by his *obiter dictum* that "no man who has anything else to do can critically read more than two or three books a month"—and of course, if you are going to allow an average of ten days to a book, the most perfect unity of purpose is inevitably going to drop out of sight.

All of this helps us to understand how it happens that Bierce, otherwise a man of intelligence, can say in all seriousness that "in England and America the art of novel writing is as dead as Queen Anne." Listen also to the following literary blasphemy:

> So far as I can judge, no good novels are now "made in Germany," nor in France, nor in any European country except Russia. The Russians are writing novels which so far as one may venture to judge . . . are in their way admirable; full of fire and light, like an opal . . . ; in their hands the novel grew great—as it did in those of Richardson and Fielding, and as it would have done in those of Thackeray and Pater if greatness in that form of fiction had been longer possible in England.

Or again:

> Not only is the novel . . . a faulty form of art, but because of its faultiness it has no permanent place in literature. In England it flourished less than a century and a half, beginning with Richardson and ending with Thackeray, since whose death no novels, probably, have been written that are worth attention.

Think for a moment what this means. Here is a man who has ventured to speak seriously about the modern novel, and who confessedly is unaware of the importance of Trollope and Meredith and Hardy, or Henry James and Rudyard Kipling and Maurice Hewlett—and who deliberately ignores the existence of Flaubert and Maupassant and Zola, Galdos and Valdes, Verga and d'Annunzio! It is not astonishing after that to find Bierce seriously questioning the value of epic poetry: "What more than they gave," he asks, "might we not have had from Virgil, Dante, Tasso, Camoens and Milton, if they had not found the epic poem ready to their misguided hands?"

The fact is that Bierce as a critic is of the iconoclastic variety. He breaks down but does not build up. He has no patience with the historical form of criticism that traces the intellectual genealogy of authorship, showing, for instance, Maupassant's debt to Poe or Bourget's debt to Stendhal. He is equally intolerant of that analytical method—the fairest of them all—that judges every written work by its author's purpose as nearly as this may be read between the lines. Nothing is more certain, he says, than if a writer of genius should bring to his task the purposes which the critics trace in the completed work, "the book would remain forever unwritten, to the unspeakable advantage of letters and morals." Yes, he tears down the recognized methods of criticism but suggests nothing better in their place. And when he himself undertakes to criticize, it is hardly ever for the purpose of paying tribute to excellence—with the noteworthy exceptions, *mirabile dictu*, of his extraordinary praise of George Stirling's poetic orgy of words, "The Wine of Wizardry." Tolstoy, for instance, he defines as a literary giant: "He has a giant's strength and has unfortunately learned to use it like a giant—which means not necessarily with conscious cruelty, but with stupidity." The journal of Marie Bashkirtseff—the last book on earth that one should expect Bierce to discuss—he sums up as "morbid, hysterical and unpleasant beyond anything of its kind in literature." Among modern critics he pronounces Howells "the most mischievous, because the ablest, of all this sycophantic crew."

The truth is that the value of Bierce as a critic lies solely in his fearlessness and downright sincerity, his unswerving conviction that he is right. He has to a rather greater extent than many a better critic the quality of consistency; and no matter how widely we are forced to disagree with his conclusions there is not one of them that does not throw an interesting side light upon Bierce, the man.

The short stories and the serious critical papers of Bierce have appeared in a spasmodic and desultory way, but from first to last he has been at heart a satirist of the school of Lucilius and Juvenal, eager to scourge the follies and the foibles of mankind at large. The fact that Bierce is absolutely in earnest, that he is destitute of fear and confessedly incorruptible accounts for the oft-repeated statement that he was for years the best-loved and the most-hated man on the Pacific Coast. Now the ability to use a stinging lash of words is all very well in itself; it is a gift that is none too common. But to be effective it must not be used too freely. The two ample volumes of Bierce's poetic invectives form a striking object lesson of the wisdom in Hamlet's contention that unless you treat men better than they deserve none will escape a whipping. And when fresh from a perusal of the contents of Shapes of Clay and Black Beetles in Amber, one has become so accustomed to seeing men flayed alive that a whole skin possesses something of a novelty. Now there is no question that there is a good deal wrong with the world, just as there always has been, if one takes the trouble to look for it. But when any one man takes upon himself the task of reprimanding the universe, it is not unreasonable that we should ask ourselves in the first instance: What manner of man is this? What are his standards and beliefs? And, if he had his way, what new lamps would he give us in place of the old? In the case of Bierce it is a little difficult to make answer with full assurance. Somewhere in his preface he has said that he has not attempted to classify his writings under the separate heads of serious, ironical, humorous and the like, assuming that his readers have sufficient intelligence to recognize the difference for themselves. But this is not always easy to do, because in a satire these different qualities and modes overlap each other so that there is always the danger of taking too literally what is really an ironical exaggeration. Here, however, is a rather significant passage taken from a serious essay entitled "To Train a Writer"— it sets forth the convictions and the general attitude toward life which Bierce believes are essential to any young author before he can hope for success—and it is only fair to infer that they represent his own personal views:

> He should, for example, forget that he is an American and remember that he is a Man. He should be neither Christian nor Jew, nor Buddhist, nor Mahometan, nor Snake Worshiper. To local standards of right and wrong he should be civilly indifferent. In the virtues, so called, he should discern only the rough notes of a general expediency; in fixed moral principles only time-saving predecisions of eases not yet before the court of conscience. Happiness should disclose itself to his enlarging intelligence as the end purpose of life; art and love as the only means to happiness. He should free himself of all doctrines, theories, etiquettes, politics, simplifying his life and mind, attaining clarity with breadth and unity with height. To him a continent should not seem wide, nor a century long. And it would be needful that he know and have an ever-present consciousness that this is a world of fools and rogues, blind with superstition, tormented with envy, consumed with vanity, selfish, false, cursed with illusions—frothing mad!

Now this strikes the average fair-minded person as a rather wholesale indictment of what on the whole has proved to be a pretty good world to live in. In fact, it is difficult to conceive of anyone honestly and literally holding so extreme a view and yet of his own volition remaining in such an unpleasant place any longer than the time required to obtain the amount of gunpowder or strychnine sufficient for an effective exit. But of course Bierce does not find life so unpleasant as he professes; in fact, he gives the impression of hugely enjoying himself by voluntarily looking out upon a world grotesquely distorted by the lenses of his imagination. He has of course a perfect right to have as much or as little faith as he chooses in any human religion or philosophy, moral doctrine or political code—only it is well when studying Bierce as a satirist and reformer to understand clearly his limitations in this respect and to discount his view accordingly. It is well, for instance, to keep in mind, when reading some of his scathing lines directed at small offenders who at most have left the world not much worse off for having lived in it, that Bierce once eulogized that wholesale destroyer of faith, Robert Ingersoll, as: "a man who taught all the virtues as a duty and a delight—who stood, as no other man among his countrymen has stood, for liberty, for honor, for good will toward men, for truth as it was given for him to see it."

To the present writer there is much that is keenly irritating in Bierce's satiric verse for the reasons above implied. It is, of course, highly uncritical to find fault with a writer for no better reason than because you find yourself out of harmony with his religious and moral faith, or his lack of it—for an author's personal beliefs should have no bearing upon the artistic value of what he produces. But putting aside personal prejudice, it may be said in all fairness that Bierce made a mistake in giving a permanent form to so large a body of his fugitive verses. It is not quite true that satiric poetry is read with the same interest after the people at whom it was directed are forgotten. Aristophanes and Horace and Juvenal cannot be greatly enjoyed today without a good deal of patient delving for the explanation of local and temporal allusions; and in modern times Pope's *Dunciad*, for instance, is probably today the least important and the least read of all his writings. It is impossible to take much interest in vitriolic attacks made twenty years ago upon various obscure Californians whose names mean nothing at all to the world at large. But, on the other had, anyone can understand and enjoy the sweeping irony as well as the shear verbal cleverness of a verse parody like "A Rational Anthem."

One is tempted to devote considerably more space than is warranted to that extremely clever collection of satiric definitions, *The Devil's Dictionary*. It represents a deliberate pose consistently maintained, it is pervaded with a spirit of what a large proportion of readers might pronounce irreverent, it tells us nothing new and can hardly be conceived of as an inspiration for higher and nobler living. But it is undeniably entertaining reading. Almost any one must smile over such specimens as the following, taken almost at random:

> MONDAY, n. In Christian countries, the day after the baseball game.
> BACCHUS, n. A convenient deity invented by the ancients as an excuse for getting drunk.
> POSITIVE, adj. Mistaken at the top of one's voice.

But it is as a writer of short stories that Bierce's future fame rests upon a firm foundation. It is not too much to say that within his own chosen field—the grim, uncompromising horror story, whether actual or supernatural—he stands among American writers second only to Edgar Allan Poe. And this is all the more remarkable when we consider his expressed scorn of new books and modern methods and his implied indifference to the development of modern technique. He does understand and consciously seeks for that unity of effect which is the foundation stone of every good short story; yet in sheer technical skill there is scarcely one among the recognizable masters of the short story today, Kipling, for instance, and the late O. Henry, Jack London and a score of his contemporaries, from whom he might not learn something to his profit. What Bierce's habits of workmanship may be the present writer does not happen to know; it is possible that he has always striven as hard to build an underlying structure, a preliminary scaffolding, for each story as Edgar Allan Poe did.

But if so he has been singularly successful in practicing the art which so artfully all things conceals. He gives the impression of one telling a story with a certain easy spontaneity and attaining his results through sheer instinct. He seldom attempts anything like a unity of time and place; and many of his short tales have the same fault which he criticizes in the modern novel: namely, that of having a panoramic quality, of being shown to us in a succession of more or less widely separated scenes and incidents.

Nevertheless, in most cases his stories are their own best justification. We may not agree with the method that he has chosen to use, but we cannot escape from the strange, haunting power of them, the grim, boding sense of their having happened—even the most weird, most supernatural, most grotesquely impossible of them—in precisely the way that he has told them.

The stories, such of them at least as really count and represent Bierce at his best, divide themselves into two groups: first, the Civil War stories, based upon his own four years' experience as a soldier during the Rebellion, and unsurpassed in American fiction for the unsparing clearness of their visualization of war. And secondly, the frankly supernatural stories contained in the volume entitled *Can Such Things Be?*—stories in which the setting is immaterial because if such things could be they would be independent of time and space. The war stories range through the entire gamut of heroism, suffering and carnage. They are stamped in all their physical details with a pitiless realism unequaled by Stendhal in the famous Waterloo episode in the *Chartreuse de Parme* and at least unsurpassed by Tolstoy or by Zola. Indeed, there is nothing fulsome or extravagant in the statement that has more than once been made that Bierce is a sort of American Maupassant. And what is most remarkable about these stories is that they never fail of a certain crescendo effect. Keyed as they are to a high pitch of human tragedy, there is always one last turn of the screw, one crowning horror held in reserve until the crucial moment. Take, for example, "A Horseman in the Sky." A sentinel whose duty it is to watch from a point of vantage overlooking a deep gorge and a vast plain beyond, to see that no scout of the Southern army shall discover a trail down the precipitous sides of the opposite slope, suddenly perceives a solitary horseman making his way along the verge of the precipice within easy range of fire. The sentinel watches and hesitates; takes aim and delays his fire. The scene shifts with the disconcerting suddenness of a modern moving picture and we see the sentinel back in his Southern home at the outbreak of the war; and we overhear the controlled bitterness of his parting with his Southern father after declaring his intention to fight for the Union. A modern story teller would consider this shifting of scene bad art; nevertheless, Bierce, in theatrical parlance, "get's it over." Back again he shifts us with a rush to the lonely horseman, shows him for a moment motionless upon the brink and the next instant launched into space, a wonderful, miraculous, awe-inspiring figure, proudly erect upon a stricken and dying horse, whose legs spasmodically continue their mad gallop throughout the downward flight to the inevitable annihilation below. This in itself, told with Ambrose Bierce's compelling art, is sufficiently harrowing, but he has something more in reserve. Listen to this:

> "Did you fire?" the sergeant whispered.
> "Yes."
> "At what?"
> "A horse. It was standing on yonder rock—pretty far out. You see it is no longer there. It went over the cliff."
> The man's face was white, but he showed no other signs of emotion. Having answered, he turned away his eyes and said no more. The sergeant did not understand.
> "See here, Druce," he said, after a moment's silence, "it's no use making a mystery. I order you to report. Was there anybody on the horse?"
> "Yes."

"Well?"
"My father."

And again, there is that extraordinary tour de force entitled "An Occurrence at Owl Creek Bridge." It is the story of a spy caught and about to be hanged by the simple expedient of allowing the board on which he stands to tilt up and drop him between the cross-beams of the bridge. The story is of considerable length. It details with singular and compelling vividness what follows from the instant that the spy feels himself dropped, feels the rope tighten around his neck and its fibers strain and snap under his weight. His plunge into the stream below, his dash for life under cover of the water, his flight, torn and bleeding, through thorns and brambles, his miraculous dodging of outposts and his passing unscathed through volleys of rapid fire, all read like a hideous nightmare—and so in fact they are, because the entire story of his rush for safety lasting long hours and days in reality is accomplished in a mere fraction of time, the instant of final dissolution—because, as it happened, the rope did not break and at the moment that he thought he had attained safety his body ceased to struggle and dangled limply beneath the Owl Creek Bridge. Variations upon this theme of the rapidity of human thought in the moment of death are numerous. There is, for instance, a memorable story by Morgan Robertson called, if memory is not at fault, "From the Main Top," in which a lifetime is crowded into the fraction of time required for the action of gravity. But no one has ever used it more effectively than Bierce.

But it is in his supernatural stories that Bierce shows even more forcefully his wizardry of word and phrase, his almost magnetic power to make the absurd, the grotesque, the impossible, carry an overwhelming conviction. He will tell you, for instance, a story of a man watching at night alone by the dead body of an old woman; a cat makes its way into the room and springs upon the corpse; and to the man's overwrought imagination it seems as though that dead woman seized the cat by the neck and flung it violently from her. "Of course you imagined it," says the friend to whom he afterwards tells the tale. "I thought so, too," rejoins the man, "but the next morning her stiffened fingers still held a handful of black fur."

For sheer mad humor there is nothing more original than the tale called "A Jug of Syrup." A certain old and respected village grocer, who through a lengthy life has never missed a day at his desk, dies and his shop is closed. One night the village banker and leading citizen on his way home drops in from force of habit at the grocery, finding the door wide open, and buys a jug of syrup, absent-mindedly forgetting that the grocer has been dead three weeks. The jug is a heavy weight to carry; yet when he reaches home he has nothing in his hand. The tale spreads like wildfire through the village and the next night a vast throng is assembled in front of the brightly lit-up grocery, breathlessly watching the shadowy form of the deceased methodically casting up accounts. One by one, they pluck up courage and make their way into the grocery—all but the banker. Riveted to the spot by the grotesque horror of the sight he stands and watches, while pandemonium breaks loose. To him in the road the shop is still brilliantly lighted but to those who have gone within it presents the darkness of eternal night and in their unreasoning fear they kick and scratch and bite and trample upon one another with the primordial savageness of the mob. And all the while the shadowy figure of the dead grocer continues undisturbed to balance his accounts.

It is a temptation to linger beyond all reason over one after another of these extraordinary and haunting imaginings, such for instance, as "Moxon's Master," in which an inventor, having made a mechanical chess-player, makes the mistake of beating it at the game and is promptly strangled to death by the revengeful puppet of his own creation. But it is impossible to do justice to all these stories separately and it remains only to single out one typical example in which perhaps he reached the very pinnacle of his strange fantastic genius, "The Death of Halpin Frayser." The theme of the story is this: it is sufficiently horrible to be confronted with a disembodied spirit, but there is one degree of horror beyond this, namely, to have to face the reanimated body of some one long dead from whom the soul has departed—because, so Bierce tells us, with the departure of the soul all natural affection, all kindliness has departed also, leaving only the base instincts of brutality and revenge. Now in the case of Halpin Frayser, it happens that the body which he is fated to encounter under these hideously unnatural conditions is that of his own mother; and in a setting as curiously and poetically unreal as any part of "Kubla Khan" he is forced to realize that this mother whom he had in life worshiped as she worshiped him is now, in spite of her undiminished beauty, a foul and bestial thing intent only upon taking his life. In all imaginative literature it would be difficult to find a parallel for this story in sheer, unadulterated hideousness.

Ambrose Bierce as a story teller may never achieve a wide popularity. His writings have too much the flavor of the hospital and the morgue. There is a stale odor of moldy cerements about them. But to the connoisseur of what is rare, unique and very perfect in any branch of fiction he must appeal strongly as one entitled to hearty recognition as an enduring figure in American letters. No matter how strongly he may offend individual convictions and prejudices with the flippant irreverence of his satiric writings, it is easy to forgive him all this and much more besides for the sake of any single one of a score or more of his best stories.

The Deterioration of the Short Story

James Lane Allen
(Interviewed by Joyce Kilmer)

Joyce Kilmer presents his interview with James Lane Allen in a conversational, almost story-like form. It is important to note that here again, both the interviewer and the interviewee appear to have given significant consideration to Edgar Allan Poe's status in American literature in general, and to his abilities as a writer of short stories in particular. See also Poe's own essay on Hawthorne's stories, and W. C. Brownell's essay on Poe, also in this volume. Beyond the issue of Poe, Allen offers his views on the effect of the Civil War upon American fiction and his reasons for believing that the first Southern literature to emerge after the war "was so mild, so tempered, so thin, so devitalized, that it seemed not to come from an enraged people, but from the memories of their ghosts." Allen's thoughts on this topic are an important acknowledgement, not only with regard to the American Civil War, but in general, of the consequences wrought upon literature by the tendency of the victorious to filter, through their own biased lens, the artistic work of the defeated. Note that Kilmer relates his own comments in paragraph form as well, with Allen's words contained in quotation marks.

That Edgar Allan Poe, in spite of his acknowledged genius, has had practically no influence on the development of the short story in America and that the current short story written in America is inferior to that written during the years between 1870 and 1895, these are two remarkable statements made to me by James Lane Allen, the distinguished author of *The Choir Invisible*, *The Mettle of the Pasture*, and many another memorable novel.

I found Mr. Allen in the pleasant workroom of his New York residence. Himself a Southerner, he is an enthusiastic admirer of the poet whose name is inseparably linked with Southern letters. But I was soon to find that he does not share the opinion of those who consider Poe the originator of the modern short story, nor does he rate Poe's influence in fiction as very wide.

"There is always much interest in short stories," he said, "among authors, and in the great body of readers. You say that Mr. Gouverneur Morris believes that except Poe almost no writer before our generation could write short stories.

"I do not wish to be placed in a position of publicly criticizing Mr. Gouverneur Morris's opinion of the short story. But it may not seem antagonistic to the opinion of any one to call attention to the fact that, of all American short stories yet written, the two most widely known in and outside our country were written independently of Poe. These are "The Man Without a Country" and "Rip Van Winkle."

"As the technique of the American short story is understood and applied today, neither of these two stories can be regarded as a work of impeccable art. But flaws have not kept them from fame. By a common verdict the flawless short stories of the day are fameless. Certainly, also, Hawthorne was uninfluenced by Poe in writing short stories that remain secure among brief American classics.

"This, of course, is limiting the outlook to our own literature. Beyond our literature, what of Balzac? In the splendor of his achievements with the novel, Balzac has perhaps been slighted as a master of the short story. Think, for instance, of such a colossal fragment as "The Atheist's Mass."

"And what of Boccaccio? For centuries before Poe, the *Decameron* shone before the eyes of the world as the golden treasury of model forms for the short story.

"And centuries before Boccaccio, flashing from hand to hand all over the world, there was a greater treasury still, the treasury of the *The Arabian Nights*.

"It is no disparagement to Poe to say that his genius did not originate the genius of the short story. His true place, his logical place, in the development of the short story is that of a man with ancestors—naturally!

"Since there is a breath of nativity blowing through his stories, I think it is the breath of far distant romance from somewhere. Certainly his stories are as remote from our civilization and from all things American as are Oriental tales."

Mr. Allen showed he had given much thought to Edgar Allan Poe's place among the American fiction writers, so I thought that he might also have some interesting things to say about Poe as a poet. He had. He mentioned a quality of Poe's verse which for some reason or other seems heretofore to have escaped the notice of students of American poetry.

"It may be worth while calling attention," he said, "to the fact that nearly all of Poe's poems belong to the night. Twelve o'clock noon never strikes to his poetic genius. His best poems are Poe's nights, if not *Arabian Nights*.

"There is a saying that the German novel long ago died of the full moon. To Poe the dead moon was the orb of life. The sun blotted him out."

Great as is his admiration for Poe's genius, Mr. Allen does not believe he has greatly influenced American prose. He said:

"As to the influence of Poe's short stories in our country this seems to be a tradition mainly fostered by professors of English in American universities and by the historians of our literature. The tradition does not prevail among American writers. Actually there is no traceable stamp of the influence of his prose writings on the work of any American short-story writer known to me, save one. That one is Ambrose Bierce."

"Why is it," I asked, "that Poe's influence on American fiction has been so slight?"

"The main reason," Mr. Allen answered, "why Poe's stories have remained outside American imitation or emulation is perhaps because they are projected outside American sympathies. They lie today where they lay when they were written—beyond the confines of what might be called the literature of the soil.

"Poe and Ambrose Bierce are at least to be linked in this: that they are the two greatest and the two coldest of all American short story writers. Any living American fictionist will perhaps bear testimony to the fact that he has never met any other writer who has been influenced by the stories of Poe."

"Mr. Allen," I said, "you believe that the American short story has not been influenced by Poe; has the American short story, however, improved since his time?"

"The renaissance of the American short story," said Mr. Allen, thoughtfully, "its real efflorescence as a natural literary art form took place at the close of the Civil War. The historians of our literature have, perhaps, as is customary with them, held to the strict continuity of tradition as explaining this renaissance. If so, they have omitted one of the instinctive forces of human nature, which invariably act in nations that have literatures and act ungovernably at the termination of all wars.

"After any war spontaneity in story telling is one of the ungovernable impulses of human nature. This can be traced from modern literature back to primitive man returning from his feuds. When he had no literature, he carved his story on the walls of his cave or on a bone to tell the glory of the fight. Before he could even carve a bone he hung up a row of the heads of the defeated. Perhaps the original form of the war short story was a good, thick volume of heads.

The Deterioration of the Short Story 115

"At the close of the American Civil War the atmosphere, both North and South, was charged with stories. The amazing fact is not that short stories should have begun at that time, but that they should have begun with such perfection. This perfection expressed itself more richly during the period, say, from 1870 to 1895—twenty-five years—than it has ever done since.

"The evidence is at hand that the best of the American short stories written during that period outweigh in value those that have been written later—with the exception of those of one person. And this evidence takes this form—that these stories were collected into volumes, had an enormous sale, had the highest critical appreciation, have passed into the histories of literature written since, have gone into the courses of English literature now being taught in the universities, and are still steadily being sold.

"Is this true of the best short stories being written now? Are any of the short stories written since that period being bound into volumes and extensively sold? Do the professors of English literature recommend them to their classes? That is the practical test.

"The one exception is O. Henry. He alone stands out in the later period as a world within himself, as much apart from anyone else as are Hawthorne and Poe."

Mr. Allen did express an opinion as to the probable effects on literature of the war. He said: "Now, the North and the South in the renaissance of the short story after the Civil War divide honors about equally. But it is impossible to speak of the Southern short story, or indeed of Southern literature at all, without being brought to the brink of a subject which lies back of the whole philosophy of Southern literature.

"Suppose that at the end of the present European war Germany should be victorious and France defeated. And suppose that in France there should not be left a single publishing house, a single literary periodical, a single literary editor, a single critic, and scarcely even a single buyer of books.

"And suppose that the defeated French people wanted to cry out their soul over their defeat and against their conquerors. And suppose that in order to do this every French novelist, short story writer, or poet, unable to keep silent, should begin to write and begin to send his novel or his short story or his poem over into Germany to be read by a German editor, published by a German publisher, and sold in a German bookshop to a German reader. What kind of French literature of the war do you think would appear in Germany and be fostered there?

"But this is exactly what happened after the war between the North and the South.

"The few voices that began to be sent northward across the demolished battle line could only be the voices that would be listened to and welcomed on the side. That is the reason why that first literature was so mild, so tempered, so thin, so devitalized, that it seemed not to come from an enraged people, but from the memories of their ghosts.

"As a result of finding war literature inexpressible in such conditions, the young generation of Southerners dropped the theme of war altogether and explored other paths. So that perhaps the most original and spontaneous fragments of this new Southern post-bellum literature are in the regions of the imagination, where no note of war is heard.

"It is not beyond the bounds of possibility that if Joel Chandler Harris, a young Southerner had possessed full freedom to wreak his genius on the war, the world might never have heard of Uncle Remus. The world might never have known that among the cotton plantations there dwelt a brother to Aesop and to La Fontaine."

The Washington Irving Country

Hamilton Wright Mabie

Washington Irving, says Hamilton Wright Mabie in this essay, "was not only the forerunner of the American novelist but the first American mythmaker." Crucial to the mythology created by Irving and his work is the environment that served both as a playground for his youthful imagination and as a backdrop for such stories as "The Legend of Sleepy Hollow" and "Rip Van Winkle." This environment is the Hudson River valley, which "penetrates Irving's work as thoroughly as the air of Ayrshire breathes through the songs of Burns." Mabie explores Irving's humor, his "metropolitan temper," and his function as a translator of Old World ideas into the lexicon of the New World. He suggests that it was Irving's "temper of the true citizen of a metropolis" that allowed him to approach literature with an easy-going type of humor that he felt had eluded other writers of the young America. Irving himself was aware that such an approach—and such subject matter as is involved in "Sleepy Hollow" and "Rip Van Winkle"—would leave his writing vulnerable to critics who would find it "light and trifling in our country of philosophers and politicians." His intention, however, was not to satisfy a critical ideal of seriousness—it was to "rub out one wrinkle from the brow of care, . . . penetrate the gathering film of misanthropy, prompt a benevolent view of human nature." It was also to create an enduring sense of place in his fiction, a sense of place that is greater than simple setting, that is as integral to the tale as the characters themselves. This is the focus of Mabie's essay, and while he may occasionally wax too romantic on the pleasantries of urban living along the way to his conclusion that Irving enriched "the Hudson with literary and personal associations, making it a place of pilgrimage," his consideration of "Washington Irving Country" marks an early critical recognition of the importance of place in the newly emerging American fiction.

Irving and Longfellow were primarily translators and interpreters of the Old World to the New; to them was due in large measure the liberation of the young nation from provincialism, not by the use of fresh motives or of novel literary forms, but by bringing the American imagination in touch with the imagination of Europe and reknitting the deeper ties which had been, in a way, severed by forcible separation from Old World rule. There was, in the first three decades of the nineteenth century, general dependence on European literature and general deference to European taste; a dependence from which Emerson and Poe, by definite and urgent teaching as well as by practice of art with that freshness and force which always form another beginning, finally effected our liberation.

This deferential attitude, this imitative spirit, had nothing in common with that assimilation of the experience, sentiment, poetic assimilation, and historic charm of the older civilization which Irving and Longfellow effected. They assisted in the emancipation from servile imitation by greatly forwarding the equalization of the conditions of culture between the Old World and the New, and by bringing the New into spiritual sympathy with the Old. This work was different from that of Emerson and Poe, but Irving and Longfellow share the distinction of breaking the formal while reuniting the vital ties, and thus preparing the way for the free interchange of influence on a basis of equality which today constitutes the rich spiritual commerce between the Old World and the New. To this great end Cooper was also a strenuous and effective worker; failing dismally when he tried the role of interpreter in *Precaution*, succeeding on original lines when he portrayed the fresh experiences and characteristic types of the new society in *The Spy* and *The Leatherstocking Tales*.

But while Irving and Longfellow were translators in a high sense and with fresh feeling of the Old World to the New, they were also original forces in the literature of the new country. Their urbanity, geniality, hospitality of mind, and sweetness of nature gave them rare sensitiveness of feeling for things old and ripe and beautiful and a winning quality of style; qualities which, among a people whose literature, during its first important period, was to carry suggestions of the pulpit with it, have tended somewhat to obscure their originality and significance. Longfellow was so gentle a preacher that, aside from a few poems so frankly didactic that we forgive their exhortations for the sake of the pure impulse they convey, the bands and gown are concealed under the singer's robes; while Irving's preaching was wholly the silent influence of one of the finest, kindliest, and truest of men. In the preponderance of ethical over artistic interests in this country Longfellow and Irving have carried less weight and made less impression than writers of more urgent ethical impulse but of far less poetic and literary power. When a great deal of current writing has been forgotten, and much that Irving and Longfellow wrote has passed into the same oblivion, it is safe to predict that "The Legend of Sleepy Hollow" and "Rip Van Winkle," and "Evangeline" and "Hiawatha," will hold their own because of their quality as literature and because they are part of the very limited legendary lore of America. Irving gave permanent form to the Knickerbocker tradition when he created Diedrich Knickerbocker and Rip Van Winkle; and in "The Legend of Sleepy Hollow" he was not only the forerunner of the American novelist but the first American mythmaker.

Like Longfellow and Cooper, he was often in Europe; and it may be suspected that when these two writers were young, and for a long time after, the new country was a lonely place for men who craved richness and beauty of life, the charm of old association, the ripeness of a society which had gotten through with foundation-laying, had built its roads, and had passed on to love things which are beautiful as well as to do things which are useful.

Born in 1783, in the cosmopolitan city of New York, where even at that early period eighteen or twenty languages were spoken, Irving went to Europe in search of health in his twenty-second year; saw something of France, Italy, Holland, and England; enjoying with the freshness of a young imagination nature, art, society, and life. "I am a young man and in Paris," he wrote to a friend at home. Returning to New York in 1806, he took his place at once in the little group of wits and men-about-town, in the good sense of the phrase, of which Paulding, Brevoort, Henry Ogden, and the Kembles were members—a spirited, vivacious company, with great capacity for enjoyment and with gifts of humor and satire which, under the influence of Goldsmith, Addison, and the eighteenth-century essayists were soon at work in the little city "to instruct the young, inform the old, correct the town, and castigate the age," to quote from *Salmagundi*, which ran its meteoric course in twenty numbers and then vanished in the mystery from which it had come. When *The History of New York by Diedrich Knickerbocker* appeared, it reminded Walter Scott of Swift and Sterne.

In 1815 Irving went to Europe for the second time, and seventeen years passed before he set foot in his native city again. During this period he wrote *The Sketch-Book*, a collection of essays, in his most characteristic vein, urbane, genial, full not only of Old World atmosphere, Old World grace, ease, mellowness of reflection, and sentiment, but full also of New World feeling. *Bracebridge Hall* brought the fragrance of old gardens and the dignity of old homes once more to the children of the men and women who had left them behind two centuries before; *The Tales of a Traveler*, which appeared two years later and was read with eager interest, dealt with old things, but was full of novelty to the untraveled America of the third decade of the last century. *The Life of Columbus* was begun, and *The Tales of the Alhambra* and *The Conquest of Granada* were finished, during this long residence abroad; and when he returned, in 1832, Irving's most characteristic work was done. He was still to write *The Life of Washington*, *Mahomet and His Successors*, the charming account of Goldsmith, and other books; but he struck no new notes and disclosed no new qualities as a writer.

At first glance it would seem as if Irving's work had been done against many backgrounds, English and Spanish as well as American, and as if his note had been cosmopolitan rather than American. The real Irving, however, was a true son of the country of which New York is the capital, and his characteristic and abiding work had behind it a city, a river, and a mountain range which were not simply the stage settings of his life, but which gave color, atmosphere, tone, to his writing. As a translator Irving rendered a great service to his country, and enriched its literature with the meditations on Westminster Abbey, the description of Stratford-on-Avon, and the group of studies of English life and landscape in *Bracebridge Hall*; but the Irving who will be known to the future will be the Geoffrey Crayon of the Knickerbocker city, and the books which will live longest, because they are in material and manner most completely his own, will be the legends of the Hudson.

His kindly and pervasive humor had as little in common with the keen, pungent New England humor as his genial and urbane spirit had with the strenuous, ethical temper of New England. The rigidity of the Puritan, the concentration of the reformer, were entirely alien to his tolerant nature. The intense feeling for the locality, the emphasis on the section, characteristic of the South from a very early period, were equally alien to him. He was a true child of the metropolis; tolerant in temper because he was on easy terms with many different races, urbane and gracious because he had found virtue and charm in many kinds of men and women, and sincerity in many kinds of religion; with a vein of deep and tender feeling running through his nature and his work, but always relieving the strain of emotion with that touch of humor which makes men kin. The qualities of the cosmopolitan city were all his; urbanity of manner, breadth of view, tolerance of temper, and a kindly, easy, genial attitude towards life.

The atmosphere of the New York of the first quarter of the nineteenth century penetrates Irving's work as thoroughly as the air of Ayrshire breathes through the songs of Burns, as lonely loveliness and the wild ruggedness of Trossachs and lakes appear and vanish and reappear in picture and vision in Scott's prose and verse, and the multitudinous murmur of waters of Cumberlandshire is heard in the poems of Wordsworth.

There was no strain of didacticism in Irving, but there was an attitude towards life which gave his work a beautiful quality of sympathy. "If, however, I can by a lucky chance, in these days of evil, rub out one wrinkle from the brow of care, or beguile the heavy heart of one moment of sadness; if I can, now and then, penetrate the gathering film of misanthropy, prompt a benevolent view of human nature, and make my reader more in good humor with his fellow-beings and himself, surely, surely I shall not then have written in vain."

This is the temper of the true citizen of a metropolis—a place where races meet and mingle on easy terms; slowly and often blindly, but none the less surely, through mutual comprehension and the tolerance that comes from it, defining in terms of experience the unity of the race and realizing the brotherhood of man. And it was still in the cosmopolitan temper that Irving wrote to a friend: "I have preferred addressing myself to the feelings and fancy of the reader more than to his judgment. My writings may appear, therefore, light and trifling in our country of philosophers and politicians. But if they possess merit in the class of literature to which they belong, it is all to which I aspire in the work."

There was something of this breadth of humor, this love of literature for itself and not as a tool for the preacher and the reformer, this old-fashioned, kindly, easy-going metropolitan temper, in the aspect and bearing of the man. "Forty years ago," writes Curtis, "upon a pleasant afternoon, you might have seen tripping with an elastic step along Broadway, in New York, a figure which even then would have been called quaint. It was a man of about sixty-six or sixty-seven years old, of a rather solid frame, wearing a Talma, as a short coat of the time was called, that hung from the shoulders, and low shoes, neatly tied, which were observable at a time when boots were generally worn. The head was slightly inclined to one side, the face was smoothly shaven, and the eyes twinkled with kindly humor and shrewdness. There was a chirping, cheery, old-school air in the whole appearance, an undeniable Dutch aspect, which, in the streets of New Amsterdam, irresistibly recalled Diedrich Knickerbocker. This modest and kindly man was the creator of Diedrich Knickerbocker and Rip Van Winkle. He was the father of our literature and at that time its patriarch."

New York was a little city of about twenty-five thousand inhabitants, living well below the site of the present City Hall, when Irving was born in a house on Williams Street, between Fulton and John, and christened in St. George's Chapel in Beekman Street. He went to school in Ann and Fulton streets, but was given more to wandering about the pier-heads and watching incoming and outgoing ships in fair weather than to orderly study. He came to know the little city intimately in its most characteristic aspects and localities; for the loitering of an imaginative child is a golden opportunity of getting at the heart of things. In this same blissful mood, while the mind was still much more concerned with the face of the world than with its own thoughts, he explored the secluded and solitary recesses of Sleepy Hollow and felt the quiet beauty of Tappan Zee on summer afternoons. A little later he made his first voyage up the Hudson on a sloop—a voyage which was then more unusual and exciting than a voyage across the Atlantic is today, and quite as long:

Of all the scenery of the Hudson," he wrote years afterwards, "the Kaatskill Mountains had the most witching effect on my boyish imagination. Never shall I forget the effect on me of my first view of them predominating over a wide extent of country, part wild, woody, and rugged; part softened away into all the graces of cultivation. As we slowly floated along, I lay on the deck and watched them through a long summer's day, undergoing a thousand mutations under the magical effects of atmosphere; sometimes seeming to approach, at other times to recede; now almost melting into hazy distance, now burnished by the setting sun, until in the evening they printed themselves against the glowing sky in the deep purple of an Italian landscape. . . . To me the Hudson is full of storied associations, connected as it is with some of the happiest portions of my life. Each striking feature brings to mind some early adventure or enjoyment; some favorite companion who shared it with me; some fair object, perchance, of youthful admiration, who, like a star, may have beamed her allotted time and passed away.

The first voyage up the river with which he will always be associated was as truly a voyage of discovery as was Hendrik Hudson's in 1609; and it was the river in its entirety, its large lines, its atmosphere, rather than its details of curving shore and climbing hill, the sweep of its powerful tide, that took possession of the boy's imagination, and became as much a part of his life of the mind and of his work as the mountains about Cadore were a part of the mind and work of Titian. It was not until April, 1835, that he purchased Sunnyside, that secluded and fragrant spot where he found such peace in his later years; and "Rip Van Winkle" had been published twelve years before its author set foot in the country which he had described more vitally than any other traveler has ever done.

From the early days of his dreaming boyhood Irving knew the river in its large outlines, its noble molding shore, its harmony of different types of landscape composed in one great picture, its atmosphere and its associations. "Rip Van Winkle" and "The Legend of Sleepy Hollow," the most original and characteristic of Irving's creations, were written in England during the period when he was transcribing with a sensitive and sympathetic hand the ripe loveliness of the English country and the rich associations of ancient structures and localities; but the Hudson valley, from the city at its conflux with the Bay to the fastnesses of the Catskills, was the background against which his imagination was working, because it was the background of his childhood.

It is now, perhaps, somewhat a matter of association, but there is a certain congruity between Irving's work and his country. In his attitude towards his fellows, his bearing in the world, Geoffrey Crayon bore the impress of the little metropolis which he has made for all time the city of the Knickerbockers; for, although Diedrich Knickerbocker has never been seen since he climbed into the Albany stage leaving his bill at the tavern unpaid, he has left his name and the tradition of his quaint personality to the great metropolis today as its one touch of mythology—a bit of fable symbolical of a past which has been buried under crushing masses of stone and iron. In the free play of Irving's imagination, in the geniality of his humor, in the ease and leisureliness of his mood, the characteristics of the larger background of his life are constantly suggested. If the Puritans had discovered the Hudson and turned its shores and current to thrifty account, it might have suggested movement, energy, the stir of active races; it suggests instead repose, quietness, long summer days of a temperature which predisposes to acceptance of what fortune brings rather than resolute grappling with adverse conditions. Sunnyside wears its name, after all these years and changes, with gracious assurance. Approached by a long shaded lane and embowered by trees, it still looks the summer in the face in the broad expanse of the Tappan Zee.

It was a happy stroke of felicitous description which called the quiet little vale where the Pocantico takes its rise Sleepy Hollow; a place as reposeful, after all these bustling and hurrying years, as it was in the days when Irving first described its pastoral somnabulance; a place not so much for meditation as for those reveries which come between sleep and awakening and add the charm of consciousness to the sensuous delight of sleep.

And although the Catskills have mass and nobility of line which produce an impression out of proportion to their actual magnitude, they have friendliness of aspect, an air of quiet hospitality, a something which eludes analysis, which imposes respect and yet invites familiarity. On summer afternoons they seem to sleep against the western sky; and a well-known artist, who has lived with them on terms of intimacy for many years, is in the habit of saying that they frame the most magnificent sunsets in the world. They stand revealed in their mystery of noble repose only in the hours when the shadows lengthen and the light loses its garishness; they are most expressive in the afternoon, when they seem sometimes to float in a mist of heat and to bound the horizon of the actual like noble visions of a world in which the light flows like molten gold. The White Mountains become bolder in the high light of morning, and invite strenuous approach and hint at great, positive rewards for the climber.

In October, the Catskills hold the very genius of the season in their keeping; so deep is the quiet that enfolds them, so rich the atmosphere in which they lie, removed at times as in a radiant mirage and again distinct in softened line and golden distance.

Mr. Curtis has said, in a pardonable poetic phrase, that the Rhine is lyrical and the Hudson epical. The Rhine is beautiful in localities, romantic, picturesque, entirely apart from their manifold associations. The Hudson is beautiful in its totality, its sustained interest, its singular harmony in diversity, its impressive continuity of changing landscapes blending into a nobly composed picture. The Rhine has a swift current and gives one a sense of movement and agitation; the Hudson flows so quietly that its very motion seems part of the stillness. On a summer day the voyage which Irving made as a boy with kindling imagination can be made between dawn and sunset, and takes one through a valley in which it seems to be always afternoon. There is activity of many kinds on either bank and on the surface of the river, but in the spaciousness of stream and landscape the hum and stir are resolved into all-embracing silence, and the quietness of Sleepy Hollow broods over wooded shores, distant hills, and flowing water.

The acquaintance with the Hudson made when Irving was a boy was renewed and deepened when he finally returned from Europe in 1832, after an absence of seventeen years. New York had grown into what seemed to him a vast city; a few years later he described it in a letter to a friend as a "great crowded metropolis . . . full of life, bustle, noise, show, and splendor, . . . one of the most racketing cities in the world." One wonders what he would think of the roaring vortex of life which the slow little town of the 1840's, when this description was written, has become in these times of rebuilding on a scale which would have appalled the magicians of the *Arabian Nights*.

Sunnyside was already old when he made it a retreat from the tumult of the city and began the process of enlargement which has adapted the ancient house to modern needs without sacrificing its old-time charm. He wrote years later:

> My own place has never been so beautiful as at present. I have made more openings by pruning and cutting down trees, so that from the piazza I have several charming views of the Tappan Zee and the hills beyond, all set, as it were, in verdant frames; and I am never tired of sitting there in my old Voltaire chair, of a long summer morning, with a book in my hand, sometimes reading, sometimes musing, and sometimes dozing, and mixing up all in a pleasant dream.

In those years when the Albany stages were making their last trips and the mild thunder of the first railroad trains began to wake the echoes of the Highlands and disturb the slumbers of the Rip Van Winkles who have never been lacking in the old towns of Dutch origin, Irving was enriching the Hudson with literary and personal associations and making it a place of pilgrimage, but his own associations with it lay far back in his boyhood. In the later years it was the background of his personal life; in his early years it was the background of his life of imagination and sentiment, of his dawning consciousness of his gifts and his vocation, of his gentle and responsive but essentially robust spirit. He lived at Sunnyside, he worshiped at Christ Church in the beautiful old village of Tarrytown, and he lies at rest in Sleepy Hollow Cemetery; these are the obvious associations of the man with the countryside which will long bear his name. To find his deeper and more vital connections with the Hudson valley one must go back to his youth, to his earlier books, to the heart of his work. Its beauty, always reposeful and in summer touched with elusive dreaminess, went home to his young imagination and reappeared again and again in charming description, in two legends which have taken their places among our classics, not only because of the charm of their form, but because they are penetrated with the very spirit of the region they portray, and in the quietness, the sensitiveness to old associations, the charity for that ease which the strenuous New England temper called by another name, the pervading humor which is never obtrusive or boisterous but is full of heart and fellowship, the happy blending of dignity and graciousness, and the modulated cadence of English speech in his work.

In the long future there may come a Hudson of new associations; a river freighted with the traffic of a valley which has become a continuous city from its mouth to the foothills of the Adirondacks. In that day some writer may appear whose work will echo the multitudinous voices of countless factories and the murmur of a vast population. But for many a year to come the Hudson which Hendrik explored as the herald of a host of Dutch settlers, the Hudson of long decades of slumberous plenty, of stately and humble homes—the Hudson of three centuries—will flow through Irving's country, and remain typical of his genius; the background of his art and life.

from The Utopian Naturalism of H. G. Wells

Stuart Pratt Sherman

This selection from Sherman's essay, written while Wells was still alive, offers one contemporary view of Wells' work. Sometimes sarcastic in tone, and always quite specific with his criticisms, Sherman describes his concept of Wells' relationship to his Victorian predecessors and of Wells' ideas in general, and then offers his critique of Wells' great desire to "bring home to the English mind a range of ideas not traditional in it." Sherman, especially through his ironic dismissals of Wells' Utopian vision, clearly aligns himself with the so-called Older Generation, and appears to be almost personally resentful of Wells' "fierce railing at conventional and customary things." Nowhere is this more clear than in his discussion of the differences between Wells' and Matthew Arnold's ideas on morality: To Arnold, "the humanistic moralist of the Victorians," the concept of morality is "a settled and simple matter." Morality is an absolute that exists outside the individual—it is a standard "to which we should vigorously subject our treacherous individual sensibilities. By adopting these principles, the individual acquires a character." To Wells and his Younger Generation, "morality is a new, complex, experimental science" that reveres none of the absolutes so firmly entrenched in the ideologies of the Older. The main defect Sherman finds here is the "lack of any principle of control" in Wells' morality, and this, indeed, is an accurate summary for all Sherman's criticisms of Wells and his work—there is too much "enthusiasm for social progress" and not enough emphasis on, nor respect for, the long-established mechanisms of social control.

It is a singularly incurious person who has never looked into the books of H. G. Wells; for through his innumerable pages swarm the figures, flash the colors, hum the voices of strictly contemporary life. Though he is on the brink of fifty, he remains the copious and incessant spokesman for the Younger Generation which he has stung into consciousness of itself. When Ann Veronica, in the novel bearing her name, announces her intention of attending an unchaperoned dance in London and spending the remnant of the night in a hotel, her aunt packs an entire "system of ideas" into the little apprehensive phrase, "But, my dear!" If you feel that the exclamation is delightfully ridiculous, you may consider yourself of the Younger Generation. If you elevate pained eyebrows with the aunt, you must set yourself down as Victorian.

When the Queen's great reign closed with her death in 1901, Wells did not go so far as to insist that the bones of her statesmen should be hung in chains and the ashes of her men of letters scattered to the winds. But he recognized, as did the court poets at the Restoration, that the readiest way to brighten a new epoch is to blacken its predecessor; violating the Victorians was an expedient justified, to adapt a military expression, by literary necessity. Accordingly he has put into circulation the popular epithets for the politics, religion, art, and morals which prevailed in the "dingy, furtive, canting, humbugging, English world" of our fathers, with its "muddled system," its "emasculated orthodoxy," its "shabby subservience," its "unreasonable prohibitions," its "meek surrender of mind and body to the dictation of pedants and old women and fools." At the same time he has been giving currency to the catchwords of the new era: "scientific method," "research," "efficiency," "cooperation," "publicity," "constructive statesmanship," "socialism," "feminism," "aviation." When we open his works of fiction, we find the Victorian muddler, the prig, the standpatter, and the prude making way for the clear-eyed theorist with the "white passion of statecraft," the titled lady with a penchant for breaking plate glass, the iconoclastic journalist in greenish-gray tweeds and art-brown tie, the independent young schoolgirl who dares to say "damn." And we are feelingly persuaded that we are moving, or that the world has rolled on and left us behind.

A writer so full of tendency as Wells, constantly setting father against son and son against father, is obviously something more or less than a novelist, quite irrespective of his sociological treatises. In the state of literary manners existing under George V, it is a bit difficult, however, to determine whether a man of letters who comes forward with a new order of ideas is a humbug or a philosopher. While I was pondering this delicate essential question in the case of Wells, there came into my hands a study of the man and his works by a critic of the younger generation, Van Wyck Brooks, which helped me out of an embarrassing situation. "Grotesque and violent as it may at first appear," says Brooks, "I believe that in the future Wells will be thought of as having played toward his own epoch a part very similar to that played by Matthew Arnold."

I was glad to be assured that Wells' air of passionate earnestness and transparent candor was not merely an aspect of his literary technique. And I seized eagerly upon the suggested parallelism; for, as I said to myself, if Wells is the Arnold of our time, by instituting a series of comparisons between the two we may measure the "march of mind" in the post-Victorian periods, and demonstrate the superiority of the ideas open to our young people over those set before their elders. But as I glanced down the page, I perceived that the likeness of Arnold and Wells was not limited to their general function in bringing home to the English mind "a range of ideas not traditional in it." That likeness extends, it seems, to "their specific attitudes toward most of the branches of thought and action they have concerned themselves with. Wells on Education, on Criticism, on Politics, and the nostrums of Liberalism; Wells, even on Religion, continues the propaganda of Arnold. Everywhere in these so superficially dissimilar writings is exhibited the same fine dissatisfaction, the same faith in ideas and standards, the same dislike of heated bungling, plunging, wilfulness, and confusion; even the same predominant contempt for most things that are, the same careful vagueness of ideal."

Though I share the critic's desire to relate Wells in some way to his predecessors, I was reluctant to acquiesce in the implications of this series of comparisons. For one point I supposed was entirely certain—that Wells repudiated the Victorians; and here was Brooks making him out the spiritual son and heir of one of their leading representatives. With a little effort, I believed, a spiritual ancestor with a more appealing likeness to his descendant could have been discovered outside the age of compromise and muddle. Arnold, as I thought, was disqualified for the relationship by characteristics which he shared with most of the reforming novelists of his sluggish period. I refer to their habit of dealing, "confusedly," no doubt, with realities, and to the modesty of their enterprises. Dickens, Kingsley, Reade, Stowe, and the rest—they did not seek to make the world over, but only to accomplish a few simple things like abolishing slavery, sweat-shops, Corn Laws, imprisonment for debt, the red tape of legal procedure, the belief in pestilence and typhoid as visitations of God—and all that sort of piddling amelioration.

What Wells required in the way of an ancestry was a man with a large free gesture, like Godwin or Rousseau sweeping away the Daedalian labyrinth of existing society, and with a few bold strokes chalking out a new social order. Shelley might serve; he was like Wells in striving "to bring home to the English mind a range of ideas not traditional in it," and he showed other points of similarity. In both Shelley and Wells we find the same fierce railing at conventional and customary things, the same eager projecting and reforming temper, the same childlike faith in the possibility of refashioning human nature, the same absorbed interest in sex, and the same abandonment of an eagerly pursued science for the sake of writing romances.

Though in these general respects Shelley was like Wells, Shelley was not in the least like Arnold, who, as will be remembered, dismissed him as a beautiful but ineffectual angel. I was thus driven to conclude that the really decisive likeness which Brooks saw between Wells and Arnold was not in their general function and temper, but in "their specific attitudes toward most of the branches of thought and action they have concerned themselves with." Yet having by this time conceived a partiality for my own literary parallel, I subconsciously ran it out alongside that of Brooks, while I was examining his contention that the prophet of the Younger Generation has continued the propaganda of the "elegant Jeremiah" of the Victorians.

Wells, we are told, continues the propaganda of Arnold with regard to education. The error involved here could have been made only in an age more concerned about its educational machinery than about its educational product. It is perfectly true that both Wells and Arnold wish the state to organize and standardize instruction. The vital question, however, is whether they agree upon what the state schools are to teach, and upon what is the "objective" of teaching.

It will hardly be disputed that if educators have anything in common it is the desire of each to reproduce his own educational species. Wells was trained at the Royal College of Science in physics, chemistry, astronomy, geology, and botany; Arnold was trained at the University of Oxford in the traditional classical disciplines. Wells belongs indubitably to the scientific species of educator, distinguished by its devotion to original research and by its steadfast belief that the crown of human endeavor is an extension of the boundaries of knowledge. Arnold belongs indubitably to the humanistic species of educator, distinguished by the importance it attaches to the assimilation of classical experience in the attainment of its highest end, the perfection of the individual character.

When Wells outlines a model course for the schools of the future, he discards Greek and Latin, and prescribes as the "backbone" of a sound curriculum as much mathematics as possible, English, and the natural sciences. When Arnold, after thirty years' experience as inspector of schools, delivers in America the essence of his educational ideas, he tells us that for most men a little mathematics suffices; that Greek will be "increasingly studied as men increasingly feel the need in them for beauty and how powerfully Greek art and literature can serve this need," and that if there is to be a separation and option between humane letters and natural sciences, the majority of men would do well "to choose to be educated in humane letters rather than in the natural sciences." For, argues Arnold, humane letters help a man's soul to get soberness, righteousness, and wisdom; while in the sphere of conduct, which is three-fourths of life, the natural sciences are comparatively impotent, leaving the moral nature undisciplined and inclined to caprice and eccentricity. Arnold maliciously cites the case of Faraday, that eminent man of science, who was a Sandemanian; one thinks also of Shelley, who emerged from his passionate study of chemistry at Oxford, declaring that the happiness of the human race depends upon the adoption of a vegetable diet; and one remembers the many heroes and heroines of Wells who have been bred on the natural sciences, and how they apply their zoological observations to the conduct of life. If, finally, we recall together the fact that Wells is a pupil and disciple of Huxley, and the fact that Arnold's *Science and Literature* is rather explicitly an attack upon the new educational programs inspired by Huxley, it should be clear that Wells came into the world to condemn the educational ideas of Arnold.

It is true that both Wells and Arnold insist upon the importance of fearless criticism—the free play of ideas upon all the subjects which concern us. But here again, before we

The Utopian Naturalism of H. G. Wells 137

agree that one continued the work of the other, it is essential to know the standpoint adopted, the method pursued, and the object contemplated by each.

At the risk of verbal absurdity one is obliged to say that Wells as critic takes his stand with the future behind him; that he retreats into the future for light on the problems of the present; and that the object of his criticism is to enable us to see things as in themselves they really are not. And, to continue the Hibernian contrast, Arnold takes his stand with the past behind him; he turns to history for light on the questions of the day, and his object, as he never tires in repeating, is to enable us to see things as in themselves they really are.

This wide difference in critical object, method, and standpoint arises from the fundamental opposition between, let us say, the pseudo-scientific and the humanistic outlook upon life. Wells—whose philosophy took shape in the biological laboratory, as under the microscope the bounds which seemed to hold individuals in fixed species disappeared and everything merged in everything else by an infinite scale of infinitesimal differences—is profoundly impressed by the uniqueness of every atom in the universe, and hence by the impossibility of formulating any law valid for any two atoms. Arnold, whose philosophy took shape as he studied the moral rather than the physical history of man, is profoundly impressed by the identity of human passions and human needs in Palestine, Greece, and England; and hence by the possibility of discovering law valid for civilized men everywhere and at all times.

We have here an explanation of the curious fact that the critic of scientific training abandons the "scientific method" and proceeds from the unknown to the known, while the critic trained in humane letters adopts the "scientific method" and proceeds from the known to the unknown. I mean that Wells, in his skepticism of the categories established by the intellect, throws reason overboard, and commits the steerage of his course to a self-willed, egoistic, anarchical imagination. "I make my beliefs," he says, "as I want them. I do not attempt to go to fact for them. I make them thus and not thus exactly as an artist makes a picture so and not so." For Arnold, who retains his faith in the intellect, truth is not something to be created, but something to be ascertained. Between the two critics yawns this gulf: Wells seeks to make whim and the will of Wells prevail, while Arnold seeks to make "right reason and the will of God" prevail.

This distinction holds between the political fantasies of Wells as set forth in his various Utopian essays, and the political and social criticisms of Arnold as set forth in his essays on Democracy, Equality, British Liberalism, and Culture and Anarchy. In the one case, a lyrical voice cries, "Come, let us drink wine, and crown our heads with roses, and break up the tedious roof of heaven into new forms." In the other case, a sober, persistent voice says, "Let us try to look at this nineteenth century of ours steadily and determine what can be done; let us straighten a little here, and level a little there, and elevate a little everywhere."

A specious likeness is perhaps observable in the fact that both Wells and Arnold advocate extending the powers of the state. The likeness itself becomes a difference the moment one reflects that Arnold recommended an increase of governmental action in a time of *laissez-faire* liberalism and radical individualism, and that Wells advocates an increase of governmental action in a time when an English statesman is telling us that "we are all socialists nowadays." It is not the function of a political critic, as Arnold reminds us, to carry coals to Newcastle.

The difference widens as soon as one considers the uses to which Wells and Arnold propose to put the enlarged powers of the state. Wells, having the courage of his sanguine imagination, desires to make the state a magnificent reservoir of science and energy and capital, "which will descend like water that the sun has sucked out of the sea," which will do away with the necessity of poverty and labor and pain, and which will abolish "the last base reason for any one's servitude or inferiority." Arnold, who prefers to retain some contact with the realities of life, phlegmatically lays down a very simple principle defining the limits of state action: "To use the state is simply to use cooperation of a superior kind. All you have to ask yourselves is whether the object for which it is proposed to use this cooperation is a rational and useful one, and one likely to be best reached in this manner. Professor Fawcett says that Socialism's first lesson is that the working-man can acquire capital without saving, through having capital supplied to him by the state, which is to serve as a fountain of wealth perennially flowing without human effort. Well, to desire to use the state for that object is irrational, vain, and mischievous. Why? Because the object is irrational and impossible."

What more need be said of the New Republic and other ships of state which Wells, like Shelley launching his paper boats on the pond in Kensington Gardens, lets drift down the stream of time? What more need be said but that Wells himself, like Shelley in his later years, has begun to despair of transforming the world by state intervention, and is transferring his faith to the redemptive power of the "beautiful moral idealisms" embodied in his own novels.

Nowhere, however, does the irreconcilable opposition of Wells and Arnold appear more distinctly than in their respective attitudes toward morality, and in particular toward "sexual morality." To Arnold, the humanistic moralist of the Victorians, morality seems a settled and simple matter. He holds that in the course of some thousands of years of civilized society the elementary principles of conduct have been adequately tested, and are now to be unequivocally accepted. They constitute a standard of "right reason" outside ourselves, to which we should vigorously subject our treacherous individual sensibilities. By adopting these principles the individual acquires a character, becomes a member of civil society, and performs the first duty of man, which is to perpetuate in and through himself the moral life of the race.

The zoological moralist of the Younger Generation holds that morality is a new, complex, experimental science with its work all before it and only a vague generalization fresh from Wells' laboratory to guide it. In order to get society upon a sound moral basis, says Wells, it is essential "to reject and set aside all abstract, refined, and intellectualized ideas as starting propositions, such ideas as right, liberty, happiness, duty, or beauty, and to hold fast to the fundamental assertion of life as a tissue and succession of births." Upon this striking obstetrical truth Wells proposes to hang Moses and all the prophets. Then he will erect upon it the new morality.

The defect in Wells' religion which distinguishes it from the religion of Arnold is exactly the defect in his morality, namely, the lack of any principle of control. Here again, he cries, we are in a field for free experimentation; nothing has been determined; "religion and philosophy have been impudent and quackish—quackish!" And so, while for Arnold religion is something which binds and limits, religion for Wells is something which looses and liberates. Arnold rejects dogmatic theology, but he writes three books to justify the Hebraic faith in an Eternal, not ourselves, which makes for righteousness, and to extol the "method" and the "sweet reasonableness" of Jesus. Wells rejects dogmatic theology; his substitute for "morality touched with emotion" is a hot fit of enthusiasm for social progress excited by fixed meditation upon the Utopian projections of his own fancy.

For Arnold, the men of true religious insight are Jesus, Marcus Aurelius, St. Francis, the author of the *Imitations*, Spinoza, who all consent together that "the Kingdom of God is within you." Wells designates this conception in the case of Marcus Aurelius as "a desire for a perfected inconsequent egoism." There is something to be said for a religion which produces a perfected egoism like that of Aurelius. But Wells, in the temper of Shelley and other social revolutionists, insists that "salvation's a collective thing," to be accomplished somewhere in the social environment, beyond the borders of the individual soul. The logical product of the sentimental altruism of Wells may be seen in the hero of almost any of his later novels—in the hero, for example, of *Tono-Bungay*, whom his creator quite accurately characterizes as a "spiritual guttersnipe in love with unimaginable goddesses."

With all its fervor for perfecting humanity in the mass, the religion of Wells somehow fails to meet the needs of the individual. It helps every one but its possessor. He has struggled with this problem, but he has not brought to his task the resources of the religious sages; he has approached it with only the resources of the scientific perfectibilians. He has felt, as we all have felt, the dumb and nameless pain which throbs at the heart of our being as we march or mince or creep or crowd through the welter of cross-purposes, wars, poverty, dreadful accidents, disease, and death, which we call our life. If you ask him how to assuage that pain, he answers that we must apply scientific methods to make mankind pacific, intelligent, well and wealthy. If you ask him why his hero, Trafford, who is already wealthy, well, intelligent, and pacific, still feels the throbbing pain, he replies, "That is because Trafford has a developed social consciousness, and cannot enter into felicity until there is a like felicity for all men to enter."

Now, did Wells possess not the insight of the religious sages, but just the sober human experience of a pagan like Horace, he would know that though all men entered his earthly paradise of lacquered ceilings, white-tiled bathrooms, scientific kitchens, motor-boats, limousines, and Victrolas, still in their poor worm-infested breasts, would dwell "black care," still would they remain spiritual guttersnipes in their scientific Elysium. And if Wells consulted Arnold or the spiritual physicians who have effectually prescribed for the essential malady of living, he would be told that inner serenity springs from self-collection, self-control, and, above all, from the Hebraic sense of personal righteousness, which is the beginning of religious wisdom.

Here and there through the works of Wells there is a glint of skepticism, a flash of self-mockery, which makes one wonder to what extent he himself feels the confidence of the young people who look to him as their savior. But I have deliberately renounced inquiry into the essential sincerity of his radicalism. I have presented him in the role that captivates his admirers, not as an empty resonator for a bewildered and discontented multitude, but as a glowing, eloquent, sanguine leader of the generation which is pressing for a place in the sun. I have exhibited him rising in adorable, unworldly innocence to arraign a social system under which two and two make only four, and water refuses to run up hill, and a child cannot eat his cake and keep it, and fire will not refrain from burning, nor the lion and the lamb lie quietly together, nor sober people take seriously his fairy tales of science, sex, and sociology. If my analysis is correct, I have detached him from Arnold, and established his connection with Shelley. This service should be grateful to him and to his followers; for I have denied him the rank of a Victorian critic only that I might elevate him to the rank of a Georgian angel.

On Mark Twain

Brander Matthews

Matthews begins his brief but telling survey of the life and works of Mark Twain with a biographical sketch, the importance of which lies in the demonstration of "the width of his experience of life," which, in turn, is important if one is to understand the "conditions under which the author has developed and the stages of his growth." Beyond the biographical matter, Matthews addresses an important and continuing issue in studies of Mark Twain. That is, to what extent is his work simply the product of a humorist whose primary interest is to entertain? Is Mark Twain to be considered a literary artist or a craftsman proficient in the provocation of laughter? In answering these questions, Matthews creates an image of Twain as a person of "sterling ethics," the "embodiment of Americanism," who eschews totalitarian dogma of any kind and seeks instead the truth, no matter how deeply or thoroughly disguised it may be. His works, from the tales to the novels to the short newspaper and magazine pieces, are then examined in the context of this image. As might be guessed, Matthews' conclusion to the foregoing issue, supported with much analysis and valuable insight, is that Twain "is to be compared with the masters of literature; and that he can abide the comparisons with equanimity."

It is a common delusion of those who discuss contemporary literature that there is such an entity as the "reading public," possessed of a certain uniformity of taste. There is not one public; there are many publics—as many in fact as there are different kinds of taste; and the extent of an author's popularity is in proportion to the number of these separate publics he may chance to please. Scott, for example, appealed not only to those who relished romance and enjoyed excitement, but also to those who appreciated his honest portrayal of sturdy characters. Thackeray is preferred by ambitious youths who are insidiously flattered by his tacit compliments to their knowledge of the world, by the disenchanted who cannot help seeing the petty meanness of society, and by those in whom sentiment has not gone to seed in sentimentality. Dickens in his own day bid for the approval of those who liked broad caricature (and were, therefore, pleased with Stiggins and Chadband), of those who fed greedily on plentiful pathos (and were, therefore, delighted with the deathbeds of Smike and Paul Dombey and Little Nell) and also those who asked for unexpected adventure (and were, therefore, glad to disentangle the melodramatic intrigues of Ralph Nickleby).

In like manner the American author who has chosen to call himself Mark Twain has attained to an immense popularity because the qualities he possesses in a high degree appeal to so many and so widely varied publics—first of all, no doubt, to the public that revels in hearty and robust fun, but also to the public which is glad to be swept along by the full current of adventure, which is sincerely touched by pathos, which is satisfied by vigorous and exact portrayal of character, which respects shrewdness and wisdom and sanity and which appreciates a healthy hatred of pretense and affectation and sham. Perhaps no one book of Mark Twain's—with the possible exception of Huckleberry Finn—is equally a favorite among his readers; and perhaps some of his best characteristics are absent from his earlier books or but doubtfully latent in them. Mark Twain is many-sided; and he has ripened in knowledge and in power since he first attracted attention as a wild Western funny man. As he has grown older he has reflected more; he has both broadened and deepened. The writer of "comic copy" for a mining-camp newspaper has developed into a liberal humorist, handling life seriously and making his readers think as he makes them laugh, until to-day Mark Twain has perhaps the largest audience of any author now using the English language. To trace the stages of this evolution and to count the steps whereby the sage-brush reporter has risen to the rank of a writer of world-wide celebrity, is as interesting as it is instructive.

I

Samuel Langhorne Clemens was born November 30, 1835, at Florida, Missouri. His father was a merchant who had come from Tennessee and who removed soon after his son's birth to Hannibal, a little town on the Mississippi. What Hannibal was like and what were the circumstances of Clemens' boyhood we can see for ourselves in the convincing pages of *Tom Sawyer*. Howells has called Hannibal "a loafing, out-at-elbows, down-at-the-heels, slave-holding Mississippi town," and the elder Clemens was himself a slave-owner, who silently abhorred slavery.

When the future author was but twelve his father died, and the son had to get his education as best he could. Of actual schooling he got little and of book-learning still less. He spent three years in the printing office of the little local paper—for, like not a few others on the list of American authors that stretches from Benjamin Franklin to William Dean Howells, he began his connection with literature by setting type. As a journeyman printer the lad wandered from town to town and rambled even as far east as New York.

When he was seventeen he went back to the home of his boyhood resolved to become a pilot on the Mississippi. How he learned the river he has told us in *Life on the Mississippi*, wherein his adventures, his experiences, and his impressions while he was a cub-pilot are recorded with a combination of precise veracity and abundant humor which makes the earlier chapters of that marvelous book a most masterly fragment of autobiography. The life of a pilot was full of interest and excitement and opportunity, and what the young Clemens saw and heard and divined during the years when he was going up and down the mighty river we may read in the pages of *Huckleberry Finn* and *Pudd'nhead Wilson*. But toward the end of the 1850's the railroads began to rob the river of its supremacy as a carrier; and in the beginning of the sixties the Civil War broke out and the Mississippi no longer went unvexed to the sea. The skill, slowly and laboriously acquired, was suddenly rendered useless, and at twenty-five the young man found himself bereft of his calling. As a border state, Missouri was sending her sons into the armies of the Union and into the armies of the Confederacy, while many a man stood doubting, not knowing which way to turn. The ex-pilot has given us the record of his very brief and inglorious service as a soldier of the South. When this escapade was swiftly ended, he went to the Northwest with his brother, who had been appointed lieutenant-governor of Nevada. Thus the man who had been born on the borderland of North and South, who had gone East as a printer, who had been again and again up and down the Mississippi, now went to the West while he was still plastic and impressionable; and he had thus another chance to increase that intimate knowledge of American life and American character which is one of the most precious of his possessions.

While still on the river he had written under the name Mark Twain, taking the name from a call of the man who heaves the lead and who cries "By the mark, three," "Mark twain," and so on. In Nevada he went to the mines and lived the life he has described in *Roughing It*, but when he failed to "strike it rich," he naturally drifted into journalism and back into a newspaper office again. The *Virginia City Enterprise* was not overmanned, and the new-comer did all sorts of odd jobs, finding time now and then to write a sketch which seemed important enough to permit of his signature. The name of Mark Twain soon began to be known to those who were curious in newspaper humor. After a while he was drawn across the mountains to San Francisco, where he found casual employment on the *Morning Call*, and where he joined himself to a little group of aspiring literators which included Bret Harte, Noah Brooks, Charles Henry Webb, and Charles Warren Stoddart.

It was in 1867 that Webb published Mark Twain's first book, *The Celebrated Jumping Frog of Calaveras*; and it was in 1867 that the proprietors of *Alta California* supplied him with funds necessary to enable him to become one of the passengers on the steamer Quaker City, which had been chartered to take a select party on what is now known as the Mediterranean trip. The weekly letters, in which he set forth what befell him on this journey, were printed in the *Alta* Sunday after Sunday, and were copied freely by the other Californian papers. These letters served as the foundation of a book published in 1869 and called *Innocents Abroad*, a book which instantly brought to the author celebrity and cash.

Both of these valuable aids to ambition were increased by his next step, his appearance on the lecture platform. Noah Brooks, who was present at his first attempt, has recorded that:

> [Mark Twain's] method as a lecturer was distinctly unique and novel. His slow, deliberate drawl, the anxious and perturbed expression of his visage, the apparently painful effort with which he framed his sentences, the surprise that spread over his face when the audience roared with delight or rapturously applauded the finer passages of his word-painting, were unlike anything of the kind they had ever known.

In the many years since that first appearance the method has not changed, although it has probably matured. Mark Twain is one of the most effective of platform-speakers and one of the most artistic, with an art of his own which is very individual and very elaborate in spite of its seeming simplicity.

Although he succeeded abundantly as a lecturer, and although he was the author the most widely-circulated book of the decade, Mark Twain still thought of himself only as a journalist; and when he gave up the West for the East, he became an editor of the *Buffalo Express*, in which he had bought an interest. In 1870 he married; and it is perhaps not indiscreet to remark that his was another of those happy unions of which there have been so many in the annals of American authorship. In 1871 he removed to Hartford, which was to be his home for thirty years; and at the same time he gave up newspaper work.

In 1872 he wrote *Roughing It*, and in the following year came his first sustained attempt at fiction, *The Gilded Age*, written in collaboration with Charles Dudley Warner. The character of Colonel Mulberry Sellers Mark Twain soon took out of this book to make him the central figure of a play, which the late John T. Raymond acted hundreds of times throughout the United States, the playgoing public pardoning the inexpertness of the dramatist in favor of the delicious humor and the compelling veracity with which the chief character was presented. So universal was this type and so broadly recognizable its traits that there were many towns in which someone accosted the actor who impersonated the ever-hopeful schemer with the declaration: "I'm the original of Sellers! Didn't Mark ever tell you? Well, he took the Colonel from me!"

Encouraged by the welcome accorded to this first attempt at fiction, Mark Twain turned to the days of his boyhood and wrote *Tom Sawyer*, published in 1875. He also collected his sketches, scattered here and there in newspapers and magazines. Toward the end of the seventies he went to Europe again with his family; and the result of this journey is recorded in *A Tramp Abroad*, published in 1880. Another volume of sketches, *The Stolen White Elephant*, was put forth in 1882; and in the same year Mark Twain first came forward as a historical novelist—if *The Prince and the Pauper* can fairly be called a historical novel. The year after he sent forth the volume describing his *Life on the Mississippi* and in 1884 he followed this with the story in which that life has been crystallized forever, *Huckleberry Finn*, the finest of his books, the deepest in its insight, and the widest in its appeal.

This *Odyssey* of the Mississippi was published by a new firm, in which the author was a chief partner, just as Sir Walter Scott had been an associate of Ballantyne and Constable. There was at first a period of prosperity in which the house issued *The Personal Memoirs of Grant*, giving his widow checks for $350,000 in 1886, and in which Mark Twain himself published *A Connecticut Yankee At King Arthur's Court*, a volume of *Merry Tales*, and a story called "The American Claimant," wherein Colonel Sellers reappears. Then there came a succession of bad years; and at last the publishing house in which Mark Twain was a partner failed, as the publishing house in which Walter Scott was a partner had formerly failed. The author of *Huckleberry Finn* was past sixty when he found himself suddenly saddled with a load of debt, just as the author of *Waverley* had been burdened full threescore years earlier; and Mark Twain stood up stoutly under it as Scott had done before him. More fortunate than Scott, Twain lived to pay the debt in full.

Since the disheartening crash came, he has given to the public a third Mississippi River tale, *Pudd'nhead Wilson*, issued in 1894; and a third historical novel, *Joan of Arc*, a reverent and sympathetic study of the bravest figure in all French history, printed anonymously in *Harper's Magazine* and then in a volume acknowledged by the author in 1896. As one of the results of a lecturing tour around the world he prepared another volume of travels, *Following the Equator*, published toward the end of 1897. Mention must also be made of a fantastic tale called "Tom Sawyer Abroad," sent forth in 1894, of a volume of sketches, *The Million Pound Bank Note*, assembled in 1893, and of a collection of literary essays, *How to Tell a Story*, published in 1897.

This is but the barest outline of Mark Twain's life—such a brief summary as we must have before us if we wish to consider the conditions under which the author has developed and the stages of his growth. It will serve, however, to show how various have been his forms of activity—printer, pilot, miner, journalist, traveler, lecturer, fiction writer, publisher— and to suggest the width of his experience of life.

II

A humorist is often without honor in his own country. Perhaps this is partly because humor is likely to be familiar, and familiarity breeds contempt. Perhaps it is partly because (for some strange reason) we tend to despise those who make us laugh, while we respect those who make us weep—forgetting that there are formulas for forcing tears quite as facile as the formulas for forcing smiles. Whatever the reason, the fact is indisputable that the humorist must pay the penalty of his humor; he must run the risk of being tolerated as a mere funmaker, not to be taken seriously, and not worthy of critical considerations. This penalty has been paid by Mark Twain. In many of the discussions of American literature he has been dismissed as though he were only a competitor of his predecessors, Artemus Ward and John Phoenix, instead of being, what he really is, a writer who is to be classed—at whatever interval only time may decide—rather with Cervantes and Moliere.

Like the heroines of the problem-plays of the modern theater, Mark Twain has had to live down his past. His earlier writing gave but little promise of the enduring qualities obvious enough in his later works. Noah Brooks has told us how he was advised if he wished to "see genuine specimens of American humor, frolicsome, extravagant, and audacious," to look up the sketches which the then almost unknown Mark Twain was printing in a Nevada newspaper. The humor of Mark Twain is still American, still frolicsome, extravagant, and audacious; but it is riper now and richer, and it has taken unto itself other qualities existing only in germ in these firstlings of his muse. The sketches in *The Jumping Frog* and the letters which made up the *Innocents Abroad* are "comic copy," as the phrase is in the newspaper offices—comic copy not altogether unlike what John Phoenix had written and Artemus Ward—better indeed than the work of these newspaper humorists (for Mark Twain had it in him to develop as they did not), but not essentially dissimilar.

And in the eyes of many who do not think for themselves, Mark Twain was only the author of these genuine specimens of American humor. For when the public has once made up its mind about any man's work, it does not relish any attempt to force it to unmake this opinion and to remake it. Like other juries, it does not like to be ordered to reconsider its verdict as contrary to the facts of the case. It is always sluggish in beginning the necessary readjustment, and not only sluggish, but somewhat grudging. Naturally it cannot help seeing the later works of a popular writer from the point of view it had to take to enjoy his earlier writings. And thus the author of *Huckleberry Finn* and *Joan of Arc* was forced to pay a high price for the early and abundant popularity of *Innocents Abroad*.

No doubt, a few of his earlier sketches were inexpensive in their elements; made of materials worn threadbare by generations of earlier funny men, they were sometimes cut in the pattern of his predecessors. No doubt, some of the earliest of all were crude and highly colored, and may even be called forced, not to say violent. No doubt, also, they did not suggest the seriousness and the melancholy which always must underlie the deepest humor, as we find it in Cervantes and Moliere, in Swift and in Lowell. But even a careless reader, skipping through the book in idle amusement, ought to have been able to see in *Innocents Abroad* that the writer of this liveliest of books of travel was no mere Merry-Andrew, grinning through a horse-collar to make sport for the groundlings; but a sincere observer of life, seeing through his own eyes and setting down what he saw with abundant humor, of course, but also with profound respect for the eternal verities.

George Eliot in one of her essays calls those who parody lofty themes "debasers of the moral currency." Mark Twain is always an advocate of the sterling ethical standard. He is ready to overwhelm an affectation with irresistible laughter, but he never lacks reverence for the things that really deserve reverence. It is not at the Old Masters that he scoffs in Italy, but rather at those who pay lip-service to things which they neither enjoy nor understand. For a ruin or a painting or a legend that does not seem to him to deserve the appreciation in which it is held he refuses to affect an admiration he does not feel; he cannot help being honest—he was born so. For meanness of all kinds he has a burning contempt; and on Abelard he pours out the vials of his wrath. He has a quick eye for all humbugs and a scorching scorn for them; but there is no attempt at being funny in the manner of the cockney comedians when he stands in the awful presence of the Sphinx. He is not taken in by the glamour of Palestine; he does not lose his head there; he keeps his feet; but he knows that he is standing on holy ground; and there is never a hint of irreverence in his attitude.

A Tramp Abroad is a better book than *Innocents Abroad*; it is quite as laughter-provoking, and its manner is far more restrained. Mark Twain was then master of his method, sure of himself, secure of his popularity; and he could do his best and spare no pains to be certain that it was his best. Perhaps there is a slight falling off in *Following the Equator*; a trace of fatigue, or weariness, or disenchantment. But the last book of travels has passages as broadly humorous as any of the first; and it proves the author's possession of a pithy shrewdness not to be suspected from a perusal of its earliest predecessor. The first book was the work of a young fellow rejoicing in his own fun and resolved to make his readers laugh with him or at him; the latest book is the work of an older man, who has found that life is not all laughter, but whose eye is as clear as ever and whose tongue is as plain-spoken.

These three books of travel are like all other books of travel in that they relate in the first person what the author went forth to see. Autobiographical also are *Roughing It* and

Life on the Mississippi, and they have always seemed to me better books than the more widely circulated travels. They are better because they are the result of a more intimate knowledge of the material dealt with. Every traveler is of necessity but a bird of passage; he is a mere carpet-bagger; his acquaintance with the countries he visits is external only; and this acquaintance is made only when he is a full-grown man. But Mark Twain's knowledge of the Mississippi was acquired in his youth; it was not purchased with a price; it was his birthright; and it was internal and complete. And his knowledge of the mining-camp was achieved in early manhood when the mind is open and sensitive to every new impression. There is in both these books a fidelity to the inner truth, a certainty of touch, a sweep of vision, not to be found in the three books of travels. For my own part I have long thought that Mark Twain could securely rest his right to survive as an author on those opening chapters in *Life on the Mississippi* in which he makes clear the difficulties, the seeming impossibilities, that fronted those who wished to learn the river. These chapters are bold and brilliant; and they picture for us forever a period and a set of conditions, singularly interesting and splendidly varied, that otherwise would have had to forego all adequate record.

III

It is highly probable that when an author reveals the power of evoking views of places and of calling up portraits of people such as Mark Twain showed in *Life on the Mississippi*, and when he has the grasp of reality Mark Twain made evident in *Roughing It*, he must needs sooner or later turn from mere fact to avowed fiction and become a story-teller. The long stories which Mark Twain has written fall into two divisions—first, those of which the scene is laid in the present, in reality, and mostly in the Mississippi Valley, and second, those of which the scene is laid in the past, in fantasy mostly, and in Europe.

As my own liking is a little less for the latter group, there is no need for me now to linger over them. In writing these tales of the past Mark Twain was making up stories in his head; personally I prefer the tales of his in which he has his foot firmly on reality. *The Prince and the Pauper* has the essence of boyhood in it; it has variety and vigor; it has abundant humor and plentiful pathos; and yet I for one would exchange the entire book for the chapter in which Tom Sawyer lets the contract for white-washing his aunt's fence.

Howells has declared that there are two kinds of fiction he likes almost equally well—"a real novel and a pure romance," and he joyfully accepts *A Connecticut Yankee at King Arthur's Court* as "one of the greatest romances ever imagined." It is a humorous romance overflowing with stalwart fun; and it is not irreverent but iconoclastic, in that it breaks not a few disestablished idols. It is intensely American and intensely nineteenth-century and intensely democratic—in the best sense of that abused adjective.

No critic, British or American, has ventured to discover any irreverence in *Joan of Arc*, wherein indeed the tone is almost devout and the humor almost too much subdued. Perhaps it is my own distrust of the so-called historical novel, my own disbelief that it can ever be anything but an inferior form of art, which makes me care less for this worthy effort to honor a noble figure. And elevated and dignified as is *Joan of Arc*, I do not think that it shows us Mark Twain at his best; although it has many a passage that only he could have written, it is perhaps the least characteristic of his works. Yet it may well be that the certain measure of success he has achieved in handling a subject so lofty and so serious helped to open the eyes of the public to see the solid merits of his other stories, in which his humor has fuller play and in which his natural gifts are more abundantly displayed.

Of these other stories three are "real novels," to use Howells' phrase; they are novels as real as any in any literature. *Tom Sawyer* and *Huckleberry Finn* and *Pudd'nhead Wilson* are invaluable contributions to American literature—for American literature is nothing if it is not a true picture of

American life and if it does not help us to understand ourselves. *Huckleberry Finn* is a very amusing volume, and a generation has read its pages and laughed over it immoderately; but it is very much more than a funny book; it is a marvelously accurate portrayal of a whole civilization. Ormsby, in an essay which accompanies his translation of *Don Quixote*, has pointed out that for a full century after its publication that greatest of novels was enjoyed chiefly as a tale of humorous misadventure, and that three generations had laughed over it before anybody suspected that it was more than a mere funny book. It is perhaps rather with the picaresque romances of Spain that *Huckleberry Finn* is to be compared than with the masterpiece of Cervantes; but I do not think that it will be a century or that it will take three generations before we Americans generally discover how great a book *Huckleberry Finn* really is, how keen its vision of character, how close its observation of life, how sound its philosophy, and how it records for us once and for all certain phases of Southwestern society which it is most important for us to perceive and to understand. The influence of slavery, the prevalence of feuds, the conditions and the circumstances that make lynchings possible—all these things are set before us clearly and without comment. It is for us to draw our own moral, each for himself, as we do when we see Shakespeare acted.

Huckleberry Finn in its art, for one thing, and also in its broader range, is superior to *Tom Sawyer* and to *Pudd'nhead Wilson*, fine as both these books are in their several ways. In no book in our language, to my mind, has the boy, simply as a boy, been better realized than in *Tom Sawyer*. In some respects *Pudd'nhead Wilson* is the most dramatic of Mark Twain's longer stories, and also the most ingenious; like *Tom Sawyer* and *Huckleberry Finn*, it has the full flavor of the Mississippi River, on which its author spent his own boyhood, and from contact with the soil of which he has always risen reinvigorated.

It is by these three novels, and especially by *Huckleberry Finn*, that Mark Twain is likely to live longest. Nowhere else is the life of the Mississippi Valley so truthfully recorded. Nowhere else can we find a gallery of Southwestern characters as varied and as veracious as those Huck Finn met in his wanderings. The histories of literature all praise the *Gil Blas* of Le Sage for its amusing adventures, its natural characters, its pleasant humor, and its insight into human frailty; and the praise is deserved. But in every one of these qualities *Huckleberry Finn* is superior to *Gil Blas*. Le Sage set the model of the picaresque novel, and Mark Twain followed his example; but the American book is richer than the French— deeper, finer, stronger. It would be hard to find in any language better specimens of pure narrative, better examples of the power of telling a story and of calling up action so that the reader cannot help but see it, than Mark Twain's account of the Shepardson-Grangerford feud, and his description of the shooting of Boggs by Sherbourn and of the foiled attempt to lynch Sherbourn afterward.

These scenes, fine as they are, vivid, powerful, and most artistic in their restraint, can be matched in the two other books. In *Tom Sawyer* they can be paralleled by the chapter in which the boy and the girl are lost in the cave, and Tom, seeing a gleam of light in the distance, discovers that it is a candle carried by Indian Joe, the one enemy he has in the world. In *Pudd'nhead Wilson* the great passages of *Huckleberry Finn* are rivaled by that most pathetic account of the weak son willing to sell his own mother as a slave "down the river." Although no one of these books is sustained throughout on this high level, and although, in truth, there are in each of them passages here and there that we could wish away (because they are not worthy of the association in which we find them), I have no hesitation in expressing here my own conviction that the man who has given us four scenes like these is to be compared with the masters of literature; and that he can abide the comparison with equanimity.

IV

Perhaps I myself prefer these three Mississippi Valley books above all Mark Twain's other writings (although with no lack of affection for those also) partly because these have the most of the flavor of the soil about them. After veracity and the sense of the universal, what I best relish in literature is this native aroma, pungent, homely, and abiding. Yet I feel sure that I should not rate him so high if he were the author of these three books only. They are the best of him, but the others are good also, and good in a different way. Other writers have given us this local color more or less artistically, more or less convincingly: one New England and another New York, a third Virginia, and fourth Georgia, and a fifth Wisconsin; but who so well as Mark Twain has given us the full spectrum of the Union? With all his exactness in reproducing the Mississippi Valley, Mark Twain is not sectional in his outlook; he is national always. He is not narrow; he is not Western or Eastern; he is American with a certain largeness and boldness and freedom and certainty that we like to think of as befitting a country so vast as ours and a people so independent.

In Mark Twain we have "the national spirit as seen with our own eyes," declared Howells; and, from more points of view than one, Mark Twain seems to me to be the very embodiment of Americanism. Self-educated in the hard school of life, he has gone on broadening his outlook as he has grown older. Spending many years abroad, he has come to understand other nationalities, without enfeebling his own native faith. Combining a mastery of the commonplace with an imaginative faculty, he is a practical idealist. No respect of persons, he has a tender regard for his fellow man. Irreverent toward all outworn superstitions, he has ever revealed the deepest respect for all things truly worthy of reverence. Unwilling to take pay in words, he is impatient always to get at the root of the matter, to pierce to the center, to see the thing as it is. He has a habit of standing upright, of thinking for himself, and of hitting hard at whatsoever seems to him hateful and mean; but at the core of him there is a genuine gentleness and honest sympathy, brave humanity and sweet kindliness.

Mark Twain has the very marrow of Americanism. He is as intensely and as typically American as Franklin or Emerson or Hawthorne. He has not a little of the shrewd common-sense and the homely and unliterary directness of Franklin. He is not without a share of the aspiration and the elevation of Emerson; and he has a philosophy of his own as optimistic as Emerson's. He possesses also somewhat of Hawthorne's interest in ethical problems, with something of the same power of getting at the heart of them; he, too, has written his parables and apologs wherein the moral is obvious and unobtruded. He is uncompromisingly honest; and his conscience is as rugged as his style sometimes is.

No American author has today at his command a style more nervous, more varied, more flexible, or more direct than Mark Twain's. His colloquial ease should not hide from us his mastery of all the devices of rhetoric. He may seem to disobey the letter of the law sometimes, but he is always obedient to the spirit. He never speaks unless he has something to say; and then he says it tersely, sharply, with a freshness of epithet and an individuality of phrase always accurate, however unacademic. His vocabulary is enormous, and it is deficient only in the dead words; his language is alive always and actually tingling with vitality. He rejoices in the daring noun and in the audacious adjective. His instinct for the exact word is not always assured, and now and again he has failed to exercise it; but we do not find in his prose the flatting and sharping he censured in Fenimore Cooper's. His style has none of the cold perfections of an antique statue; it is too modern and to American for that, and too completely the expression of the man himself, sincere and straightforward. It is not free from slang, although this is far less frequent than one might expect; but it does its work swiftly and cleanly. And it is capable of immense variety. Consider the tale of "The Blue Jay" in *A Tramp Abroad*, wherein the humor is sustained by unstated pathos; what could be better told than this, with every word the right word and in the right place? And take Huck Finn's description of the storm when he was alone on the island, which is in dialect, which will not parse, which bristles with double negatives, but which none the less is one of the finest passages of descriptive prose in all American literature.

V

After all, it is as a humorist pure and simple that Mark Twain is best known and best beloved. In the preceding pages I have tried to point out the several ways in which he transcends humor, as the word is commonly restricted, and to show that he is no mere fun-maker. But he is a fun-maker beyond all question, and he has made millions laugh as no other man of our century has done. The laughter he has aroused is wholesome and self-respecting; it clears the atmosphere. For this we cannot but be grateful. As Lowell said, "let us not be ashamed to confess that, if we find the tragedy a bore, we take the profoundest satisfaction in the farce. It is a mark of sanity." There is no laughter in Don Quixote, the noble enthusiast whose wits are unsettled; and there is little on the lips of Alceste, the misanthrope of Molière; but for both of them life would have been easier had they known how to laugh. Cervantes himself, and Molière also, found relief in laughter for their melancholy; and it was the sense of humor which kept them tolerantly interested in the spectacle of humanity, although life had pressed hardly on them both. On Mark Twain also life has left its scars; but he has bound up his wounds and battled forward with a stout heart, as Cervantes did, and Molière. It was Molière who declared that it was a strange business to undertake to make people laugh; but even now, after two centuries, when the best of Molière's plays are acted, mirth breaks out again and laughter overflows.

It would be doing Mark Twain a disservice to compare him to Molière, the greatest comic dramatist of all time; and yet there is more than one point of similarity. Just as Mark Twain began by writing comic copy which contained no prophesy of a masterpiece like *Huckleberry Finn*, so Molière was at first the author only of semi-acrobatic farces on the Italian model in no wise presaging *Tartuffe* and *The Misanthrope*. Just as Molière succeeded first of all in pleasing the broad public that likes robust fun, and then slowly and step by step developed into a dramatist who set on the stage enduring figures plucked out of the abounding life about him, so also has Mark Twain grown, ascending from *The Jumping Frog* to *Huckleberry Finn*, as comic as its elder brother and as laughter-provoking, but charged also with meaning and with philosophy. And like Molière again, Mark Twain has kept solid hold of the material world; his doctrine is never sublimated into sentimentality. He sympathizes with the spiritual side of humanity, while never ignoring the sensual. Like Molière, Mark Twain takes his stand on common-sense and thinks scorn of affectation of every sort. He understands sinners and strugglers and weaklings; and he is not harsh with them, reserving his scorching hatred for hypocrites and pretenders and frauds.

At how long an interval Mark Twain shall be rated after Molière and Cervantes it is for the future to declare. All that we can see clearly now is that it is with them that he is to be classed.

On Gogol

William Lyon Phelps

Phelps here declares Gogol the "self-conscious founder of Russian realism." This judgment, which remains valid even as we approach century's end, may at first seem odd to American and Western-European readers who are most familiar with his stories "The Cloak" (or "The Overcoat") and "The Nose," and who, when they think of realism, think of Balzac (see George Brandes' essay on Balzac, also in this volume) or Dreiser. The subject matter of "The Cloak" and "The Nose" is not realistic in the sense that the events described could possibly occur outside a fictional realm. Rather, their realism lies in their detailed portraits of character and scene and dramatic interaction, while the narrative itself may venture into decidedly unrealistic, even supernatural, territory. Phelps explores Gogol's realism in this essay, comparing it to other Russian works and to the English and French varieties of realistic fiction as well. His lament that Gogol was little known outside Russia, in the years since this essay's composition, has been answered to a great extent—Gogol and his works, particularly *Revizor*, *Dead Souls*, and several short stories, have come to be known not only as Russian classics, but as masterpieces in world literature (though the massive popularity his works continue to enjoy in Russia remains elusive in the world at large). Phelps' essay is a useful biographical, historical, and critical study of Gogol and his milieu, a useful introduction to the writer whose appearance on the scene was, in Phelps' words, "a literary sunrise."

Nikolai Vassilievich Gogol was born at Sorotchinetz, in Little Russia, in March, 1809. The year in which he appeared on the planet proved to be the literary *annus mirabilis* of the century; for in that same year were born Charles Darwin, Alfred Tennyson, Abraham Lincoln, Poe, Gladstone, and Holmes. His father was a lover of literature, who wrote dramatic pieces for his own amusement, and who spent his time on the old family estates, not in managing the farms, but in wandering about the fields, and beholding the fowls of the air. The boy inherited much from his father; but, unlike Turgenev, he had the best of all private tutors, a good mother, of whom his biographer says, *Elle demeure toujours sa plus intime amie.*

At the age of twelve, Nikolai was sent away to the high school at Nezhin, a town near Kiev. There he remained from 1821 to 1828. He was an unpromising student, having no enthusiasm for his lessons, and showing no distinction either in scholarship or deportment. Fortunately, however, the school had a little theatre of its own, and Gogol, who hated mathematics, and cared little for the study of modern languages, here found an outlet for all his mental energy. He soon became the acknowledged leader of the school in matters dramatic, and unconsciously prepared himself for his future career. Like Schiller, he wrote a tragedy, and called it *The Robbers*.

I think it is probable that Gogol's hatred for the school curriculum inspired a passage in *Taras Bulba*, though here he ostensibly described the pedagogy of the fifteenth century:

> The style of education in that age differed widely from the manner of life. These scholastic, grammatical, rhetorical, and logical subtleties were decidedly out of consonance with the times, never had any connection with and never were encountered in actual life. Those

who studied them could not apply their knowledge to anything whatever, not even the least scholastic of them. The learned men of those days were even more incapable than the rest, because they were farther removed from all experience.

In December, 1828, Gogol took up his residence in St. Petersburg, bringing with him some manuscripts that he had written while at school. He had the temerity to publish one, which was so brutally ridiculed by the critics, that the young genius, in despair, burned all the unsold copies — an unwitting prophecy of a later and more lamentable conflagration. Then he vainly tried various means of subsistence. Suddenly he decided to seek his fortune in America, but he was both homesick and seasick before the ship emerged from the Baltic, and from Lubeck he fled incontinently back to Petersburg. Then he tried to become an actor, but lacked the necessary strength of voice. For a short time he held a minor official position, and a little later was professor of history, an occupation he did not enjoy, saying after his resignation, "Now I am a free Cossack again." Meanwhile his pen was steadily busy, and his sketches of farm life in the Ukraine attracted considerable attention among literary circles in the capital.

Gogol suffered from nostalgia all the time he lived at St. Petersburg; he did not care for that form of society, and the people, he said, did not seem like real Russians. He was thoroughly homesick for his beloved Ukraine, and it is significant that his short stories of life in Little Russia, truthfully depicting the country customs, were written far off in a strange and uncongenial environment.

In 1831 he had the good fortune to meet the poet Pushkin, and a few months later in the same year he was presented to Madame Smirnova; these friends gave him the *entrée* to the literary salons, and the young author, lonesome as he was, found the intellectual stimulation he needed. It was Pushkin who suggested to him the subjects for two of his most famous works, *Revizor* and *Dead Souls*. Another friend, Jukovski, exercised a powerful influence, and gave invaluable aid at several crises of his career. Jukovski had translated the *Iliad* and the *Odyssey*; his enthusiasm for Hellenic poetry was contagious; and under this inspiration Gogol proceeded to write the most Homeric romance in Russian literature, *Taras Bulba*. This story gave the first indubitable proof of its author's genius, and today in the world's fiction it holds an unassailable place in the front rank. The book is so short that it can be read through in less than two hours; but it gives the same impression of vastness and immensity as the huge volumes of Sienkiewicz.

Gogol followed this amazingly powerful romance by two other works, which seem to have all the marks of immortality: the comedy *Revizor*, and a long, unfinished novel, *Dead Souls*. This latter book is the first of the great realistic novels of Russia, of which *Fathers and Children*, *Crime and Punishment*, and *Anna Karenina* are such splendid examples.

From 1836 until his death in 1852, Gogol lived mainly abroad, and spent much time in travel. His favorite place of residence was Rome, to which city he repeatedly returned with increasing affection. In 1848 he made a pilgrimage to the Holy Land, for Gogol never departed from the pious Christian faith taught him by his mother; in fact, toward the end of his life, he became an ascetic and a mystic. The last years were shadowed by illness and—a common thing among Russian writers—by intense nervous depression. He died at Moscow, 21 February 1852. His last words were the old saying, "And I shall laugh with a bitter laugh." These words were placed on his tomb.

Most Russian novels are steeped in pessimism, and their authors were men of sorrows. Gogol, however, has the double distinction of being the only great comic writer in the language, and in particular of being the author of the only Russian drama known all over the world, and still acted everywhere on the Continent. Although plays do not come within the scope of this book, a word or two should be said about this great comedy; for *Revizor* exhibits clearly the double nature of the author,—his genius for moral satire and his genius for pure fun. From the moral point of view, it is a terrible indictment against the most corrupt bureaucracy of modern times; from the comic point of view, it is an uproarious farce.

The origin of the play is as follows: while travelling in Russia one day, Pushkin stopped at Nizhni-Novgorod. Here he was mistaken for a state functionary on tour among the provinces for purposes of government inspection. This amused the poet so keenly that he narrated all the circumstances to Gogol and suggested that the latter make a play with this experience as the basis of the plot. Gogol not only acted on the suggestion, but instead of a mere farce, he produced a comedy of manners. Toward the end of his life he wrote: "In *Revizor* I tried to gather in one heap all that was bad in Russia, as I then understood it; I wished to turn it all into ridicule. The real impression produced was that of fear. Through the laughter that I have never laughed more loudly, the spectator feels my bitterness and sorrow." The drama was finished on the fourth of December 1835, and of course the immediate difficulty was the censorship. How would it be possible for such a satire either to be printed or acted in Russia? Gogol's friend, Madame Smirnova, carried the manuscript to the Czar, Nikolas I. It was read to him; he roared with laughter, and immediately ordered that it be acted. We may note also that he became a warm friend of Gogol, and sent sums of money to him, saying nobly, "Don't let him know the source of these gifts; for then he might feel obliged to write from the official point of view."

The first performance was on the 19 April 1836. The Czar attended in person, and applauded vigorously. The success was immediate, and it has never quitted the stage. Gogol wrote to a friend: "On the opening night I felt uncomfortable from the very first as I sat in the theatre. Anxiety for the approval of the audience did not trouble me. There was only one critic in the house—myself—that I feared. I heard clamorous objections within me which drowned all else. However, the public, as a whole, was satisfied. Half of the audience praised the play, the other half condemned it, but not on artistic grounds."

Revizor is one of the best-constructed comedies in any language; for not only has it a unified and well-ordered plot, but it does not stop with the final fall of the curtain. Most plays by attempting to finish up the story with smooth edges, leave an impression of artificiality and unreality, for life is not done up in such neat parcels. The greatest dramas do not solve problems for us, they supply us with questions. In *Revizor*, at the last dumb scene, after all the mirth, the real trouble is about to begin; and the spectators depart, not merely with the delightful memory of an evening's entertainment, but with their imagination aflame. Furthermore, *Revizor* has that combination of the intensely local element with the universal, so characteristic of works of genius. Its avowed attempt was to satirize local and temporal abuses; but it is impossible to imagine any state of society in the near future where the play will not seem real. If Gogol had done nothing but write the best comedy in the Russian language, he would have his place in literature secure.

His first book, *Evenings on a Farm near the Dikanka (Veillees de l'Ukraine)*, appeared early in the thirties, and, with all its crudity and excrescences, was a literary sunrise. It attracted immediate and wide-spread attention, and the wits of Petersburg knew that Russia had an original novelist. The work is a collection of short stories or sketches, introduced with a rollicking humorous preface, in which the author announces himself as Rudii Panko, raiser of bees. Into this book the exile in the city of the North poured out all his love for the country and the village customs of his own Little Russia. He gives us great pictures of nature, and little pictures of social life. He describes with the utmost detail a country fair at the place of his birth, Sorotchinetz. His descriptions of the folk, the animals, and the bargainings seem as true as those in *Madame Bovary*—the difference is in the attitude of the author toward his work. Gogol has nothing of the aloofness, nothing of the scorn of Flaubert; he himself loves the revelry and the superstitions he pictures, loves above all the people. Superstition plays a prominent role in these sketches the unseen world of ghosts and apparitions has an enormous influence on the daily life of the peasants. The love of fun is everywhere in evidence; these people cannot live without practical jokes, violent dances and horse-play. Shadowy forms of amorous couples move silent in the warm summer night, and the stillness is broken by silver laughter. Far away, in his room at St. Petersburg, shut in by the long winter darkness, the homesick man dreamed of the vast landscape he loved, in the warm embrace of the sky at noon, or asleep in the pale moonlight. The first sentence of the book is a cry of longing. "What ecstasy; what splendor has a summer day in Little Russia!" Pushkin used to say that the Northern summer was a caricature of the Southern winter.

The *Evenings on a Farm* indicates the possession of great power rather than consummate skill in the use of it. Full of charm as it is, it cannot by any stretch of language be called a masterpiece. Two years later, however, Gogol produced one of the great prose romances of the world, *Taras Bulba*. He had intended to write a history of Little Russia and a history of the Middle Ages, in eight or nine volumes. In order to gather material, he read annals diligently, and collected folk-lore, national songs, and local traditions. Fortunately out of this welter of matter emerged not a big history, but a short novel. Short as it is, it has been called an epic poem in the manner of Homer, and a dramatization of history in the manner of Shakespeare. Both remarks are just, though the influence of Homer is the more evident; in the descriptive passages, the style is deliberately Homeric, as it is in the romances of Sienkiewicz, which owe so much to this little book of Gogol. It is astonishing that so small a work can show such colossal force. Force is its prime quality—physical, mental, religious. In this story the old Cossacks, centuries dead, have a genuine resurrection of the body. They appear before us in all their amazing vitality, their love of fighting, of eating and drinking, their intense patriotism, and their blazing devotion to their religious faith. Never was a book more plainly inspired by passion for race and native land. It is one tremendous shout of joy. These Cossacks are the veritable children of the steppes, and their vast passions, their Homeric laughter, their absolute recklessness in battle, are simply an expression of the boundless range of the mighty landscape:

> The further they penetrated the steppe, the more beautiful it became. Then all the South, all that region which now constitutes New Russia, even to the Black Sea, was a green, virgin wilderness. No plow had ever passed over the immeasurable waves of wild growth; the horses alone, hiding themselves in it as in a forest, trod it down. Nothing in nature could be finer. The whole surface of the earth presented itself as a green-gold ocean, upon which were sprinkled millions of different flowers. Through the tall, slender stems of the grass peeped light-blue, dark-blue, and lilac star-thistles; the yellow broom thrust up its pyramidal head; the parasol-shaped white flower of the false flax shimmered on high. A wheat-ear, brought God knows whence, was filling out to ripening. About their slender roots ran partridges with out-stretched necks. The air was filled with the notes of a thousand different birds. In the sky, immovable, hung the hawks, their wings outspread, and their eyes fixed intently on the grass. The cries of a cloud of wild ducks, moving up from one side, were echoed from God knows what distant lake. From the grass arose, with measured sweep, a gull, bathed luxuriously in blue waves of air. And now she has vanished on high, and appears only as a black dot; now she has turned her wings, and shines in the sunlight. Deuce take you, steppes, how beautiful you are!

The whole book is dominated by the gigantic figure of old Taras Bulba, who loves food and drink, but who would rather fight than eat. Like so many Russian novels, it begins at the beginning, not at the second or third chapter. The two sons of

Taras, wild cubs of the wild old wolf, return from school, and are welcomed by their loving father, not with kisses and affectionate greeting, but with a joyous fist combat, while the anxious mother looks on with tears of dismayed surprise. After the sublime rage of fighting, which proves to the old man's satisfaction that his sons are really worthy of him, comes the sublime joy of brandy, and a prodigious feast, which only the stomachs of fifteenth century Cossacks could survive. Then despite the anguish of the mother—there was no place for the happiness of women in Cossack life—comes the crushing announcement that on the morrow all three males will go off to the wars, from which not one of them will return. One of the most poignant scenes that Gogol has written is the picture of the mother, watching the whole night long by her sleeping sons—who pass the few hours after the long separation and before the eternal parting, in deep, unconscious slumber.

The various noisy parliaments and bloody combats are pictured by a pen alive with the subject; of the two sons, one is murdered by his father for preferring the love of a Capulet to the success of the Montagues; the other, Ostap, is taken prisoner, and tortured to death. Taras, in disguise, watches the appalling sufferings of his son; just before his death, Ostap, who had not uttered a word during the prolonged and awful agony, cries out to the hostile sky, like the bitter cry *My God, why hast thou forsaken me?* "Father! where are you? Do you hear all?" and to the amazement of the boy and his torturers, comes, like a voice from heaven, the shout, "I hear!"

Fearful is the vengeance that Taras Bulba takes on the enemy; fearful is his own death, lashed to a tree, and burned alive by his foes. He dies, merrily roaring defiant taunts at his tormentors. And Gogol himself closes his hero's eyes with the question, "Can any fire, flames, or power be found on earth, which are capable of overpowering Russian strength?"

In its particular class of fiction, *Taras Bulba* has no equal except the Polish trilogy of Sienkiewicz; and Gogol produces the same effect in a small fraction of the space required by the other. This is of course Romanticism rampant, which is one reason why it has not been highly appreciated by the French critics. And it is indeed as contrary to the spirit of Russian fiction as it is to the French spirit of restraint. It stands alone in Russian literature, apart from the regular stream, unique and unapproachable, not so much one of the great Russian novels as a soul-thrilling poem, commemorating the immortal Cossack heart.

Gogol followed up the *Evenings on a Farm near the Dikanka* with two other volumes of stories and sketches, of which the immortal *Taras Bulba* was included in one. These other tales show an astonishing advance in power of conception and mastery of style. I do not share the general enthusiasm for the narrative of the comically grotesque quarrel between the two Ivans: but the three stories, "Old-fashioned Farmers," "The Portrait," and "The Cloak," show to a high degree that mingling of fantasy with reality that is so characteristic of this author. The obsolete old pair of lovers in "Old-fashioned Farmers" is one of the most charming and winsome things that Gogol wrote at this period: it came straight from the depths of his immeasurable tenderness. It appealed to that pity which, as every one has noticed, is a fundamental attribute of the national Russian character. In "The Portrait," which is partly written in the minute manner of Balzac, and partly with the imaginative fantastic horror of Poe and Hoffmann, we have the two sides of Gogol's nature clearly reflected. Into this strange story he has also indicated two of the great guiding principles of his life: his intense democratic sympathies, and his devotion to the highest ideals in art. When the young painter forsakes poverty and sincerity for wealth and popularity, he steadily degenerates as an artist and eventually loses his soul. The ending of the story, with the disappearance of the portrait, is remarkably clever. The brief tale called "The Cloak" or "The Overcoat" has great significance in the history of Russian fiction, for all Russian novelists have been more or less influenced by it. Its realism is so obviously and emphatically realistic that it becomes exaggeration, but this does not lessen its tremendous power: then suddenly at the very end, it leaves the ground, even the air, and soars away into the ether of romance.

Although these stories were translated into English by Hapgood over twenty years ago, they have produced very little impression anywhere outside of Russia. This is a misfortune for the world, for Gogol was assuredly one of the great literary geniuses of the nineteenth century, and he richly repays attentive reading. In Russia he has been appreciated, immensely respected and admired, from the day that he published his first book; but his lack of reputation abroad is indicated by the remark of Mr. Baring in 1910, "the work of Gogol may be said to be totally unknown in England." This statement is altogether too sweeping, but it counts as evidence.

Despite Gogol's undoubted claim to be regarded as the founder of Russian fiction, it is worth remembering that of the three works on which rests his international fame, two cannot possibly be called germinal. The drama *Revizor* is the best comedy in the Russian language; but, partly for that very reason, it produced no school. The romance *Taras Bulba* has no successful follower in Russian literature, and brought forth no fruit anywhere for fifty years, until the appearance of the powerful fiction-chronicles by Sienkiewicz. It has all the fiery ardor of a young genius; its very exaggeration, its delight in bloody battle, show a certain immaturity; it breathes indeed the spirit of youth. With the exception of "The Cloak," Gogol had by 1840 written little to indicate the direction that the best part of Russian literature was to take. It was not until the publication of *Dead Souls* that Russia had a genuine realistic novel. This book is broad enough in scope and content to serve as the foundation of Russian fiction, and to sustain the wonderful work of Turgenev, Tolstoi, and Dostoevski. All the subsequent great novels in Russia point back to *Dead Souls*.

No two books could possibly show a greater contrast than *Taras Bulba* and *Dead Souls*. One reveals an extraordinary power of condensation: the other an infinite expansion. One deals with heroes and mighty exploits; the other with positively commonplace individuals and the most trivial events. One is the revival of the glorious past; the other a reflection of the sordid present. One is painted with the most brilliant hues of Romanticism, and glows with the essence of the Romantic spirit—aspiration; the other looks at life through an achromatic lens, and is a catalogue of realities. To a certain extent, the difference is the difference between the bubbling energy of youth and the steady energy of middle age. For, although Gogol was still young in years when he composed *Dead Souls*, the decade that separated the two works was for the author a constant progress in disillusion. In the sixth chapter of the latter book, Gogol has himself revealed the sad transformation that had taken place in his own mind, and that made his genius express itself in so different a manner:

> Once, long ago, in the years of my youth, in those beautiful years that rolled so swiftly, I was full of joy, charmed when I arrived for the first time in an unknown place; it might be a farm, a poor little district town, a large village, a small settlement: my eager, childish eyes always found there many interesting objects. Every building, everything that showed an individual touch, enchanted my mind, and left a vivid impression. Today I travel through all the obscure villages with profound indifference, and I gaze coldly at their sad and wretched appearance: my eyes linger over no object, nothing grotesque makes me smile: that which formerly made me burst out in a roar of spontaneous laughter, and filled my soul with cheerful animation, now passes before my eyes as though I saw it not, and my mouth, cold and rigid, finds no longer a word to say at the very spectacle which formerly possessed the secret of filling my heart with ecstasy. O my youth! O my fine simplicity!

Gogol spent the last fifteen years of his life writing this book, and he left it unfinished. Pushkin gave him the subject, as he had for *Revizor*. One day, when the two men were alone together, Pushkin told him, merely as a brief anecdote, of an unscrupulous promoter, who went about buying up the names of dead serfs, thus enabling their owners to escape payment of the taxes which were still in force after the last registration. The names were made over to the new owner, with all legal formalities, so that he apparently possessed a large fortune, measured in slaves; these names the promoter transferred to a remote district, with the intention of obtaining a big cash loan from some bank, giving his fictitious property as security; but he was quickly caught, and his audacious scheme came to nothing. The story stuck in Gogol's mind, and he conceived the idea of a vast novel, in which the travels of the collector of dead souls should serve as a panorama of the Russian people. Both Gogol and Pushkin thought of *Don Quixote*, the spirit of which is evident enough in this book.

Not long after their interview, Gogol wrote to Pushkin: "I have begun to write *Dead Souls*. The subject expands into a very long novel, and I think it will be amusing, but now I am only at the third chapter. I wish to show, at least from one point of view, all Russia." Gogol declared that he did not write a single line of these early chapters without thinking how Pushkin would judge it, at what he would laugh, at what he would applaud. When he read aloud from the manuscript, Pushkin, who had listened with growing seriousness, cried "God! what a sad country is Russia!" and later he added, "Gogol invents nothing; it is the simple truth, the terrible truth."

The first part of his work, containing the first eleven chapters, or "songs," was published in May 1842. For the rest of his life, largely spent abroad, Gogol worked fitfully at the continuation of his masterpiece. Ill health, nervous depression, and morbid asceticism preyed upon his mind; in 1845 he burned all that he had written of the second volume. But he soon began to rewrite it, though he made slow and painful progress, having too much of the *improductivé slave* either to complete it or to be satisfied with it. At Moscow, a short time before his death, in a night of wakeful misery, he burned a whole mass of his manuscripts. Among them was unfortunately the larger portion of the rewritten second part of *Dead Souls*. Various reasons have been assigned as the cause of the destruction of his book—some have said, it was religious remorse for having written the novel at all; others, rage at adverse criticism; others, his own despair at not having reached ideal perfection. But it seems probable that its burning was simply a mistake. Looking among his papers, a short time after the conflagration, he cried out, "My God! what have I done! That isn't what I meant to burn!" But whatever the reason, the precious manuscript was forever lost and the second part of the work remains sadly incomplete, partly written up from rough notes left by the author, partly supplied by another hand.

Dead Souls is surely a masterpiece, but a masterpiece of life rather than of art. Even apart from its unfinished shape, it is characterized by that formlessness so distinctive of the great Russian novelists—the sole exception being Turgenev. The story is so full of digressions, of remarks in mock apology addressed to the reader, of comparisons of the Russian people with other nations, of general disquisitions on realism, of glowing soliloquies in various moods, that the whole thing is a kind of colossal note-book. Gogol poured into it all his observations, reflections, and comments on life. It is not only a picture of Russia, it is a spiritual autobiography. It is without form, but not void. Gogol called his work a poem; and he could not have found a less happy name. Despite lyrical interludes, it is as far removed from the nature and form of poetry as it is from drama. It is a succession of pictures of life, given with the utmost detail, having no connection with each other, and absolutely no crescendo, no movement, no approach to a climax. The only thread that holds the work together is the person of the traveling promoter, Chichikov, whose visits to various communities give the author the opportunity he desired. After one has grasped the plan of the book, the purpose of Chichikov's mission, which one can do in two minutes, one may read the chapters in any haphazard order. Fortunately they are all interesting in their photographic reality.

The whole thing is conceived in the spirit of humour, and its author must be ranked among the great humorists of all time. There is an absurdity about the mission of the chief character, which gives rise to all sorts of ludicrous situations. It takes time for each serf-owner to comprehend Chichikov's object, and he is naturally regarded with suspicion. In one community it is whispered that he is Napoleon, escaped from St. Helena, and traveling in disguise. An old woman with whom he deals has an avaricious cunning worthy of a Norman peasant. The dialogue between the two is a masterly commentary on the root of all evil. But although all Russia is reflected in a comic mirror, which by its very distortion emphasizes the defects of each character, Gogol was not primarily trying to write a funny book. The various scenes at dinner parties and at the country inns are laughable; but Gogol's laughter, like that of most great humorists, is a compound of irony, satire, pathos, tenderness, and moral indignation. The general wretchedness of the serfs, the indifference of their owners to their condition, the pet30iness and utter meanness of village gossip, the ridiculous affectations of small-town society, the universal ignorance, stupidity, and dullness—all these are remorselessly revealed in the various bargains made by the hero.

And what a hero. A man neither utterly bad nor very good; shrewd rather than intelligent; limited in every way. He is a Russian, but a universal type. No one can travel far in America without meeting scores of Chichikovs: indeed he is an accurate portrait of the American promoter, of the successful commercial traveler, whose success depends entirely not on the real value and usefulness of his stock-in-trade, but on his knowledge of human nature and the persuasive power of his tongue. Chichikov is all things to all men.

Not content with the constant interpolation of side remarks and comments, queries of a politely ironical nature to the reader, in the regular approved fashion of English novels,

Gogol added after the tenth chapter a defiant epilogue, in which he explained his reasons for dealing with fact rather than with fancy, of ordinary people rather than with heroes, of commonplace events rather than with melodrama; and then suddenly he tried to jar the reader out of his self-satisfaction, like Balzac in *Père Goriot*.

> Pleased with yourselves more than ever, you will smile slowly, and then say with grave deliberation: "It is true that in some of our provinces one meets very strange people, people absolutely ridiculous, and sometimes scoundrels too!"
> Ah, but who among you, serious readers, I address myself to those who have the humility of the true Christian, who among you, being alone, in the silence of the evening, at the time when one communes with oneself, will look into the depths of his soul to ask in all sincerity this question? "Might there not be in me something of Chichikov?"

This whole epilogue is a program—the program of the self-conscious founder of Russian Realism. It came from a man who had deliberately turned his back on Romanticism, even on the Romanticism of his friend and teacher, Pushkin, and who had decided to venture all alone on a new and untried path in Russian literature. He fully realized the difficulties of his task, and the opposition he was bound to encounter. He asks and answers the two familiar questions invariably put to the native realist. The first is, "I have enough trouble in my own life: I see enough misery and stupidity in the world: what is the use of reading about it in novels?" The second is, "Why should a man who loves his country uncover her nakedness?"

Gogol's realism differs in two important aspects from the realism of the French school, whether represented by Balzac, Flaubert, Guy de Maupassant, or Zola. He had all the French love of veracity, and could have honestly said with the author of *Une Vie* that he painted *l'humble verite*. But there are two ground qualities in his realistic method absent in the four

French writers: humour and moral force. Gogol could not repress the fun that is so essential an element in human life, any more than he could stop the beating of his heart; he saw men and women with the eyes of a natural born humorist, to whom the utter absurdity of humanity and human relations was enormously salient. And he could not help preaching, because he had boundless sympathy with the weakness and suffering of his fellow-creatures, and because he believed with all the tremendous force of his character in the Christian religion. His main endeavor was to sharpen the sight of his readers, whether they looked without or within; for not even the greatest physician can remedy an evil, unless he knows what the evil is.

Gogol is the great pioneer in Russian fiction. He had the essential temperament of all great pioneers, whether their goal is material or spiritual. He had vital energy, resolute courage, clear vision, and an abiding faith that he was traveling in the right direction. Such a man will have followers even greater than he, and he rightly shares in their glory. He was surpassed by Turgenev, Dostoevski, and Tolstoi, but had he lived, he would have rejoiced in their superior art, just as every great teacher delights in being outstripped by his pupils. He is the real leader of the giant three, and they made of his lonely path a magnificent highway for human thought. They all used him freely: Tolstoi could hardly have written *The Cossacks* without the inspiration of Gogol, Turgenev must have taken the most beautiful chapter in *Virgin Soil* directly from "Old-fashioned Farmers," and Dostoevski's first book, *Poor Folk*, is in many places almost a slavish imitation of "The Cloak"—and he freely acknowledged the debt in the course of his story. The uncompromising attitude toward fidelity in art which Gogol emphasized in "The Portrait" set the standard for every Russian writer who has attained prominence since his day. No one can read Chekhov and Andreev without being conscious of the hovering spirit of the first master of Russian fiction. He could truthfully have adapted the words of Joseph Hall:

> I first adventure: follow me who list,
> And be the second Russian Realist.

from On Balzac

George Brandes

This selection from George Brandes' essay is rich in details on Balzac's personal life, the theories and inspiration behind his fiction, and contemporary reaction to his work. Such items as an anecdote from his friend Gautier and an excerpt from Goethe's diary giving his response to Balzac's work lend a knowing specificity to this portrait of the author who's grand scheme was to unite the great mass of his works into a single masterpiece, *The Human Comedy*. Much like Nikolai Gogol's attempt to show "all Russia" in his *Dead Souls* (see Phelps' essay on Gogol, also in this volume), Balzac, in *The Human Comedy*, intended to present France in all its diversity by the methodical accumulation of fictional detail on thousands of characters in nearly as many settings. Brandes' essay offers a clear description of Balzac's process, treating along the way Balzac's view of marriage, his ideas on virtue and vice, and his thoughts on what he calls the "epic of middle class life, of destinies to which no poet has turned his attention."

Balzac was bound to fail in his attempt to rival Gautier in the latter's special province for this reason: that he sees and feels in a perfectly different way. Gautier the stylist is an artist of the first rank, but Gautier the author, in spite of his poetic qualities, is cold and at times arid. His talent may be defined as the talent of the plastic artist who has won a place for himself in literature. Balzac, on the other hand, is an inferior stylist, but an author of the highest rank. He cannot place his characters before us with a few telling words, because he does not himself see them in one single plastic situation. When, conjured up by his imagination, they present themselves to the eye of his mind, he sees them, not gradually, but at once, in different stages of their lives and in different costumes; he comprehends their whole career; he observes all the multitude of their peculiar movements and gestures, and hears the sound of their voices in utterances so characteristic that they bring the speaker bodily before us. It is not, as in the case of the stylist, a single picture, the result of a single, perhaps subtle, but somewhat dry association of ideas, which reveals the character to us; no, Balzac's character is composed of a hundred thousand associations of ideas which unconsciously blend and form a unit, complicatedly rich as nature itself, as that real human unit, which consists of a strange mixture of innumerable physical and spiritual elements. It would require a whole book to give a sufficient number of examples of Balzac's incomparable power of bringing personalities vividly before us by means of their manner of expressing themselves, or even simply by some peculiarity in their dress, their household arrangements, and the like. His difficulty lay in the proper disposal of the wealth of material which his memory and his inspirations thrust upon him. At one time he would compress too many ideas, the association between which was intelligible to himself alone, into a few words (as when he says of an innocent, unoffending lady that "her ears were the ears of the slave and the mother"); at another, he would write down, one after the other, all the observations and fancies which his prolific brain suggested every time he invented a fictitious personage, and lose himself in a diffuse, descriptive, argumentative flow of words, which conveyed no distinct impression to the reader — the reason being that the electric communication between the organs of poetic vision and poetic eloquence in the author's brain was faulty, and at times altogether broken off. Ten-fold labor had to supply the bitterly felt deficiency.

When we remember that, in those days of collaboration, Balzac never had a collaborator, never even a copyist, we can understand what patience and what stupendous exertion were required to produce, in the course of twenty years, the novels, tales, and plays, more than a hundred in number, which proceeded from his pen.

While Hugo writes as the artists of the Renaissance painted, surrounded by a company of youthful admirers and pupils, Balzac sits alone in his study. He allows himself little sleep. He goes to bed between seven and eight, gets up again at midnight and works in his white Dominican monk's habit, with a gold chain round his waist, until daybreak, when, feeling the want of exercise, he rushes off himself to the printer's to deliver his manuscript and correct proofs. His is no ordinary proof-correcting. He demands eight or ten impressions of each sheet. This is partly because he is not certain of having found the final, correct expressions, but also because it is his habit to complete the general outline of his story first, and fill in the details by degrees. Half, sometimes more than half, the payment he receives, goes into the pocket of the printer; but not even extreme need will induce him to allow his work to appear before it seems to him as perfect as he can make it. He is the despair of the type-setter, but his proof-reading is also his own most painful task. The first impression is set with wide spaces between the paragraphs, and gigantic margins; and both of these are by degrees filled to overflowing. When he has done with it, the page, with its dots and dashes, strokes and stars, looks like a picture of a firework. Then the heavily built, untidily dressed man with the crushed felt hat and the sparkling eyes, hurries home along the crowded street, every here and there respectfully made way for by some one who knows or guesses him to be a genius. More hours of work follow. Before dinner he seeks recreation in a call on a lady, or a raid on the old curiosity shops in search of a rare piece of furniture or an old painting. Not till evening comes again does this indefatigable worker think of rest.

Gautier writes:

> Sometimes he would come to my house in the morning, groaning, exhausted, dizzy with the fresh air, like a Vulcan escaped from his forge, and fling himself down on the sofa. His long night's work had made him ravenously hungry, and he would pound sardines and butter into a kind of paste which reminded him of a dish he had been accustomed to at home, and which he ate spread upon bread. This was his favorite food. As soon as he had eaten he would fall asleep, begging me, before he closed his eyes, to wake him in an hour. Paying no attention to this request, I took care that no noise in the house should disturb this well-earned slumber. When he awoke at last and saw the evening twilight spreading its grey shadows over the sky, he would jump up and overwhelm me with abuse, call me traitor, robber, murderer. I had been the means of his losing 10,000 francs, for he would have earned as much as that with the novel which he would have planned if he had been awake, even leaving possible second and third editions out of the question; I was causing the most terrible catastrophes and most inconceivable complications; I had made him miss appointments with financiers, publishers, duchesses; he would not be in a position to meet his engagements; this fatal sleep would cost him millions. I was consoled by seeing the fresh Touraine color returning to his cheeks.

When, taking Charles de Lovenjoul's bibliographical work as a guide, we follow Balzac's labors week by week; when we see from his own letters how, never allowing himself to be distracted by those Parisian gaieties in which he nevertheless often took part, nor to be scared by the literary cannonades of his frequently envious critics, he steadily, stone by stone, raised the pyramid of his life's work, determined to make it as broad and as high as possible, we are inspired by a feeling of respect for the man and his courage. The good-natured, stout, noisy Balzac was no Titan; indeed, in that generation of heaven-storming Titans and Titanesses he appears a peculiarly earth-bound creature. But he is of the race of the Cyclops; he was a mighty master-builder who worked with a giant's strength; and the uncouth, brick-laying, carpentering Cyclops raised his building as high as the two great lyric geniuses of the day, Victor Hugo and George Sand, mounted on their wings.

He had never any doubt of his own ability. A self-confidence which corresponded to his talent, and which sometimes displayed itself in naive boastfulness, but never in petty vanity, carried him bravely through all the trials and struggles of the first years; and in the moments of depression which occurred in his, as they do in every artist's life, he was, as we understand from his letters, comforted and strengthened by faithful, secret love. A woman whose name he never mentioned to his friends, whom he only alludes to with reverence as "an angel," "a moral sun," and who to him was "more than a mother, more than a friend, more than one human being can be to another," supported him with her self-sacrificing devotion, with word and deed, in the many troubles which beset his youth. We know that he was acquainted with her in 1822, and for twelve years (she died in 1837) she managed from time to time "to steal away from duty, family, society, all the hampering ties of Parisian life," and spend two hours with him. Balzac, always ardent in his praise, naturally employs the strongest expressions where he loves; what is really worthy of notice is the delicacy of feeling displayed by this man, who is so invariably decried for his cynical sensuality—the admiration and gratitude in which his love takes shape.

Balzac's earliest literary model was Sir Walter Scott, an author of whom he can never have reminded any one, and with whom, when his genius reaches its maturity, he has hardly anything in common. The writer of the *Comedie Humaine* was a man of far too modern a spirit to be able to remain faithful to historic fiction. He felt no home-sickness for any past century; he had amassed a vast wealth of observation, and involuntarily chose themes in which he could turn this to the best account. He was dimly conscious that the writer of historical novels, unless he be content simply to thrust the characters which he has before him as models into antiquated costumes, must take his modern, personal, psychological observations, and, as it were, force them back into a more primitive age—a difficult task, the attempt at which seldom resulted in more than a thinly disguised reproduction of the manners and customs of the writer's contemporaries, or at any rate of their ideas. It was not in Balzac's nature to collect information laboriously from old chronicles; he studied the living men and women of his own day.

La Physiologie du Marriage, the first of his works to arouse attention, supplemented Brillat-Savarin's harmless *Physiologie du Gout* with a half-jocose, half-scientific, wholly coarse analysis of that institution of society which French literature from time immemorial has treated as a butt for witticisms, an object of ironical homage, and a matter for unsparing investigation. Balzac regards it in the light of a tragi-comic social necessity, defends it, and assists it with good advice in its struggle with those destructive elements, masculine and feminine caprices and passions. Marriage has a special attraction for Balzac as being the battle-ground of two egoisms; he rushes with the ruthlessness of a wild boar through its boundless domain of attractions and repulsions, snuffing and poking his nose into everything. In France marriage has always been a tolerably external, public matter; it need not surprise us that Balzac has little reverence for its mysteries. He writes of them with Moliere's outspokenness, but less healthily—more pessimistically and more grossly. The book is full of clever, coarse conceits and laughable anecdotes, and is often extremely amusing from the contrast between the frivolous, licentious matter and the professorial or father-confessor style in which it is expounded by the youthful lecturer on the science of marriage. It is, nevertheless, an immature production of a writer who has been early robbed of all beautiful illusions. *Le Physiologie du Marriage* reveals none of Balzac's nobility of thought and delicacy of feeling—nothing but his gift of ruthless, searching analysis.

It would seem as if the opening of his authorial vein in this book had freed him for a long time from bad blood. His conception of life is henceforward a more elevated one, or rather, it divides itself into two conceptions, a serious and a sportive. The serious and the sensually cynic philosophy of human life, which in *La Physiologie du Marriage* blended into one repulsive whole, now separate, displaying themselves in the form of tragedy and satirical comedy. In 1831 he both writes his first philosophic novel, *La Peau de Chagrin* (which laid the foundation of his fame as an author) and begins, with *La belle Imperia*, the long series of the *Contes drolatiques*, a collection of tales in the freest Renaissance style, reminiscent of Queen Marguerite and Brantome in matter and of Rabelais in language. Told in the language of our own day, they would be both disgusting and dull; but the grand, simple, old-fashioned prose style, which lends more nobility to the subject than even the severest metrical forms, transforms these deifications of the flesh into genuine works of art as burlesque as the tales told by one of those worldly-minded, handy, jovial monks who swarm in the legendary lore of every country.

In one of the masterly prologues to this collection of tales the author tells how, having lost his patrimony in his youth, and being reduced to the direst poverty, he cried to heaven, like the woodcutter in the fable who had lost his axe, in hopes that the gods might take pity on him and give him another axe. What Mercury threw down to him was an ink-horn, on which were engraved the three letters AVE. He stood turning the heavenly gift round and round, in his hands until he caught sight of the letters backwards, EVA. What was Eva? What but all women in one? A heavenly voice had called to him: "Think of woman; she will heal thy woes and fill thy pockets; she is thy fortune. Ave, I salute thee! Eva, O woman!" Which, being interpreted, meant that what he was now to attempt was to win a smile from the unprejudiced reader by mad and merry love stories. And he succeeded. In none of his other writings did his style attain such brilliance and vigour; Rubens' coloring is not bolder nor richer, and Rubens hardly equals this herculean wantonness with his fauns and drunken bacchanalians. But it is difficult to find ten successive lines that are fit for quotation or reading aloud.

La Peau de Chagrin is Balzac's first literary tussle with the reality of his age; it is a spirited, many-sided work, rich in germs and shoots; and with its fine, simple symbols it anticipates that almost comprehensive picture of modern society which its author was to give to the world in his complete works. The externalities of modern life, such as the theatre and the fashionable lady's boudoir; the dissatisfied and hopeless poverty of the talented young author thrown into relief by the orgies of wealthy journalists and women of the demi-monde; the contrast, in the two principal female characters, between the worldly and the loving heart—all this is shown us in a strange, fantastic light. The book consists of a few connected gaudy spectacular scenes; there is more reflection and symbolic art than plastic talent in it. The youthful hero, who is on the point of committing suicide in despair over his hopeless poverty, receives from an aged dealer in curiosities a piece of wild ass' skin, on which neither steel nor fire produces the smallest effect, and which secures to its possessor the fulfillment of his every wish, but which shrinks a line or two with the gratification of each; simultaneously with the final disappearance of the ass' skin the life of its owner comes to an end. The persuasive powers of a marvellous imagination have succeeded in imparting credibility to the supernatural part of this profound allegory. Balzac has given the fantastic element in it a form which permits of its blending with the modern realistic elements. Aladdin's lamp, when it was rubbed, instantly worked in a direct miracle; even in Oehlenschlager's *Aladdin* it supersedes the law of cause and effect. Not so the ass' skin; it does nothing directly; it only ensures the fortunate issue of events, steadily shrinking the while. It seems to be made of the fabric of which our lives are composed. The gradual annihilation of the human being is brought about, we are told, by two instinctive actions, which exhaust its sources of life. *Deux verbes experiment toutes les formes que prennent ces deux causes de mort: vouloir et pouvoir. Vouloir nous brule et pouvoir nous detruit.* That is to say, we die at last because we go on killing ourselves every day.

The ass' skin is, like ourselves, at last annihilated by "*vouloir et pouvoir.*" With real profundity Balzac shows in this powerful representation of the chief impulse of the younger generation of his day—to drink the cup of life greedily to the very dregs—what emptiness there is in satiety, how certain it is that death lies cowering in the satisfaction of desire. Youthful, fertile, suggestive, and vaguely melancholy, like all books produced by genius before the acquirement of personal experience, *La Peau de Chagrin* made its mark abroad as well as in France. Goethe read it during the last year of his life. Riemer (who attributes the authorship of the book to Victor Hugo) reports Goethe to have said on October 11, 1831:

> I have been reading more of *La Peau de Chagrin*. It is an excellent work in the newest style, distinguished by the vigor and cleverness of its back-and-forward movement between the impossible and the painful, and by the logical manner in which the marvelous is employed in producing the most extraordinary chains of thought and events, of which, taken in detail, much that is favorable might be said.

In a letter of the 17th November of the same year he writes of the same work: "This book, the production of an intellect of very high order, points to a deep-seated, incurable corruption in the French nation, which will spread steadily unless the provinces, which can neither read nor write, restore it to health again, as far as that is possible."

The novel contains not a little autobiography. Balzac knew from his own experience the feelings of the impecunious youth, who, descending from his garret, picks his way in his solitary pair of white silk stockings and dancing-shoes across the muddy street, in deadly fear of being splashed by a passing carriage, and consequently deprived of the sight of his beloved. But what interests us more is the sum of inward experience which is contained in the book, and which amounts to this: Society detests misfortune and suffering, avoids them like infectious diseases, never hesitates in choosing between a misfortune and a crime. Let a misfortune be never so sublime, society will manage to belittle it, to make it ridiculous by some witty sally; it has no sympathy to spare for the fallen gladiator. To Balzac, in short, even now in his youth, society appears devoid of every higher religious or moral feeling; it shrinks from the old, the sick, and the poor; it does homage to luck, to strength, and, above all, to wealth; it tolerates no misfortune out of which it cannot by some means or other coin money.

Before Balzac's day the novel had occupied itself almost exclusively with one theme—love; but the god of Balzac's contemporaries was money; therefore in his books money, or rather the lack of money, the desire of money, is the pivot on which society turns. The idea was audacious and novel. To enter in a work of fiction, a romance, into accurate details regarding the incomes and expenditure of the principal characters, in short, to treat money as of prime importance, was a perfectly new departure; and many denounced it as prosaic, even coarse; for it is always considered coarse to say what every one thinks, and what consequently all have tacitly agreed to conceal or to prevaricate about—and especially coarse to proclaim it in an art which is often regarded as the art of beautiful lying.

One day in 1836 Balzac appeared in his sister's room in the wildest of spirits. Imitating the gestures of a drum-major with his thick cane (on the cornelian handle of which was engraved in Turkish a sultan's motto: "I am the destroyer of obstacles"), he shouted to her during the pauses of an accompaniment of martial music made with his tongue: "Congratulate me, little one, for I am on the point of becoming a genius." He had conceived the idea of combining all his novels, those already published and those yet to be written, into one great work—*La Comedie Humaine*.

The plan was stupendous and perfectly original; nothing of the kind existed in any known literature; it was a product of the same genius for systematization which at the beginning of his career had inspired him with the idea of writing a series of historical romances embracing a succession of centuries. But this was a far more interesting and fertile idea. For, if the work were successful, it would possess the same force of illusion as if it dealt with historic facts, and it would, moreover, not merely be a little fragment of life symbolically and artistically enlarged into an image of the whole, but might justly lay claim to be, in the scientific sense of the word, a whole. In the *Divina Commedia*, Dante had, as it were, focused all the philosophy and experience of life in the Middle Ages. His ambitious rival proposed giving to the world by means of two to three thousand characters, which each represented hundreds of others, a complete psychology of all the different classes of French society, and thus, indirectly, of his age. It is undeniable that the result was something unique.

Balzac's fictional country has, like the real country, its ministers, its judges, its generals, its financiers, manufacturers, merchants, and peasants. It has its priests, its town and country doctors, its men of fashion, its painters, sculptors, and designers, its poets, prose authors, and journalists, its old and its newly created aristocracy, its vain and unfaithful, and its lovable and its victimized wives. And the illusion is astonishing and complete.

The personages reappear in one after another of the numerous novels; we make acquaintance with them in all the different stages of their lives; they are constantly being alluded to by other characters when they do not appear themselves; the descriptions of their appearance, dress, homes, habits, and daily life are as minute and exact as if they had been given by a dressmaker, a doctor, a tradesman, or a lawyer, and at the same time so vivid that we feel as if we must certainly find the person described either in the street and house indicated as his home, or else paying a call upon the distinguished lady whose salon is the rendezvous of all the people of fashion in the novels. It seems almost impossible that these beings, one and all, should be mere figments of the brain; we involuntarily think of the France of that day as peopled by them.

And it is the whole of France. For Balzac described in their turn towns and districts in every part of the country. Far from despising the provinces, he took a pride in displaying his intimate knowledge of all the peculiarities of their stagnant life, of their virtues, all culminating in resignation, and their vices, the offspring of narrow-mindedness. But Paris in a very special manner lives in his pages. And Balzac's Paris is not the old city of Notre-Dame de Paris, the picturesque, medieval capital with its marked social contrasts, its animated street life, and its superstitious ecclesiasticism; still less is it Victor Hugo's ideal Paris, that impossible New Jerusalem of intellect and enlightenment; it is the real modern city with its joy, its sorrow, and its shame—the entrancing wonder of our own age, which throws the trappings of antiquity into the shade—the gigantic polypus with the hundred thousand tentacles which drags everything, near and far, into its clutches—the great cancer eating into France. The Paris of the author's own day lives in his books, with its narrow streets, of which he gives Rembrandt-like etchings, with its rattle and shrieks, its street cries in the early morning and its mighty evening chorus of voices—a sea of sound which he reproduces for us with an orchestral effect, reminding us of the men initiated into the mysteries of old, who seemed to have eaten drums and drunk cymbals. Balzac knows about everything in Paris—the architecture of the houses, the furniture of the rooms, the pedigrees of the fortunes, the successive owners of the valuable objects of art, the ladies' *toilettes*, the dandies' tailor bills, the lawsuits which divide families, the state of health, means of subsistence, needs, and desires of all the different classes of the population. He had absorbed the town through every pore. Contemporary novelists sought refuge from the mist-veiled sun of Paris, and the commonplace modern Parisian, in Spain, or Africa, or the East; but to Balzac no sun was fairer than that which shone on Paris. Those about him endeavored to conjure forth the shades of a distant or departed beauty: but to him ugliness was no more repulsive than the nettle is to the botanist, the snake to the zoologist, or disease to the doctor. He would never, in Faust's place, have called Helen from the grave; he would have been much more likely to send for his friend, the Prefect of Police, or the criminal, and get him to tell tales of what he had gone through and seen and heard.

By dint of observation he amasses an enormous collection of separate traits, and the cataloguing of these traits frequently makes the introductory part of his novels tiresome and confusing; at the end of an interminable description of a house, a figure, a face, a nose, the reader sees nothing, is simply bored. But then comes a moment when the author's glowing imagination melts and fuses together all these commonplace elements presented to it by his faithful memory, as Benvenuto Cellini melted down plates and spoons and from them cast his Perseus. Goethe says (in his diary of February 26, 1780):

> The collecting and putting together of details does not help me to understand. But after I have long occupied myself in dragging together sticks and straws, and have attempted to warm myself in vain, although there is fire at the heart of the heap and smoke everywhere, suddenly the flame springs up and the whole is in a blaze.

In Balzac's novels the descriptive parts are often smothered in smoke, but the flame never fails to burst forth.

For Balzac was not merely an observer; he was a seer. If he happened to meet a workman and his wife going home from the theatre between eleven and twelve at night, he as likely as not followed them the whole way to their little house beyond the outer boulevards. He heard them talk (the mother dragging their child after her by the hand) first of the play, then of their own affairs. They talked of the money that was to be paid them next day, spending it in imagination in twenty different ways, quarreling during the process and revealing their characters in the squabble. And Balzac listened so intently to their complaints of the length of the winter, the dearness of potatoes, the rise in the price of turf, that he at last lived their life, and, as we are told in his *Facino Cane*, "felt their rags upon his back and walked with his feet in their soleless shoes." Their dreams, their necessities, entered into his soul, and he went about in a kind of waking dream. Whilst this mental intoxication lasted he gave up all his usual habits and became something different from himself, became the age. He did not only write his stories, he lived them; his fictitious characters were so vividly present to him that he spoke of them to his acquaintances as if they actually existed. When he undertook a journey to a place he wished to describe, he would say: "I am going to Alençon, where Mademoiselle Carmon lives; to Grenoble, where Dr. Benassis lives." He used to give his sister the news of his imaginary world. "Do you know who it is Felix de Vandenesse is marrying? A Mademoiselle de Bellefeuille. It is a good match, in spite of all Mademoiselle de Bellefeuille has cost the family." One day when Jules Sandeau was speaking of his sister, who was ill, Balzac, who had been listening absently for some time, suddenly said: "This is all very well, my friend; but now to return to realities—let us talk of Eugenie Grandet." It was necessary that the illusion in his own case should be as strong as this, if he was to communicate it to others with approximate strength. His imagination had the commanding power which allows no doubt to arise. It exercised this quality in practical matters too. Among the hundreds of projects which occurred to him as possible means of freeing himself from debt, was that of covering the bare fields surrounding the little country-house of *Les Jardies* (which he had bought that he might have a security to give his mother) with enormous forcing-houses, which, because of the entire absence of shelter from the sun's rays, would require very little artificial heat. In these forcing-houses a hundred thousand pineapples were to be grown, which, sold at five francs each, instead of at the ordinary price of twenty, would yield the fortunate grower a yearly income of 400,000 francs "without his requiring to produce a scrap of manuscript." With such convincing eloquence did the originator of this plan demonstrate the absolute certainty of its success, that his friends actually looked out for a shop on one of the boulevards for the retail of the pineapples, and consulted him as to the form and color of the signboard. At another time he was firmly persuaded, I know not upon what grounds, that he had discovered the place in the outskirts of Paris where Toussaint Louverture had buried his treasure; and so successful was he in communicating his belief to his friends Sandeau and Gautier, neither of them particularly simple-minded persons, that these two gentlemen armed themselves with spades and stole like criminals out of Paris at five o'clock in the morning to dig at the spot indicated—naturally to find nothing. The expression, "the power of imagination," is peculiarly applicable in Balzac's case.

And this imagination which prevailed over others was his own tyrant. It gave him no peace. Not satisfied with the conception of plans, with the sweet, but barren joy of artistic dreams, it compelled him to be continually carrying out his plans, to keep himself in that habit of producing, without which inspiration so soon vanishes.

When, writing in *La Cousine Bette* of the gifted sculptor Wenceslas Steinbock's idleness, he quotes these words of "a great writer": "I sit down to my work with despair and rise from it with sorrow," he is obviously in a half-modest way quoting himself. And he adds:

> If the artist does not fling himself, without reflecting, into his work, as Curtius flung himself into the yawning gulf, as the soldier flings himself into the

enemy's trenches, and if, once in this crater, he does not work like a miner on whom the walls of his gallery have fallen in; if he contemplates difficulties instead of overcoming them one by one, he is simply looking on at the suicide of his own talent.

The method of production which he describes is his own, but it is not the only, not even the highest method. More tranquil, less modern spirits have kept their heads clear and their eyes undimmed above the seething crater of their work; and by doing so have preserved a sound critical sense which has prevented them from ever becoming as tediously entangled in their material as the author of *Le Cure de Village* and *Le Medicin de Campagne*. But, on the other hand, a certain dull glow, a thrilling, enthralling something which has become a necessity to modern nerves, is too often lacking in their works.

In the long preface to the *Comedie Humaine* Balzac sets forth his intentions and his aim. He begins by expressing his contempt for the usual method of writing history. "In reading those dry and most unattractive registers of events which go by the name of history, we observe," he writes, "that the historians of all countries and ages have forgotten to give us the history of morals." This deficiency he intends, as far as it lies in his power, to supply. He purposes producing a record of the passions, virtues, and vices of society by condensing kindred characters into types—thus, with patience and perseverance, writing the book which Rome, Athens, Tyre, Memphis, and Persia "have unfortunately neglected to bequeath to us." We see what a low opinion Balzac has of history. His extremely slight acquaintance with it made it easier for him to be contemptuous. Nor was he himself really the historian of his age; he was, to use his own striking and correct expression, its naturalist. He followed the lead of Geoffrey St. Hilaire, who demonstrated the unity of structure of all the different species. Among scientists he felt himself a scientist, a professor of sociology:

Society produces from man, according to environment, as many different men as there are species in zoology. The difference between soldier, laborer, official, lawyer, idler, scientist, statesman, merchant, sailor, poet, priest, is, though more difficult to grasp, quite as great as the difference between wolf, lion, horse, raven, shark, seal, and cow.

The analogy is not complete, partly because, as Balzac himself immediately admits, the wife and husband of society do not always correspond to each other as do the male and female of the zoologist, partly because it is in the power of the social individual to pass from one class or calling to another, whereas in nature transition from one species to another is impossible during the lifetime of an individual.

What Balzac really means, and what is perfectly true, is that the standpoint from which he views society corresponds exactly, as a rule, to the standpoint from which the scientist investigates nature. He never moralizes and condemns; he never, in this unlike most of his fellows, allows himself to be led by disgust or enthusiasm to describe otherwise than truthfully; to him, as to the naturalist, nothing is too small, nothing too great to be examined and explained. Seen through the microscope, the spider is larger and more complicatedly organized than the hugest elephant; regarded from the scientific standpoint, the majestic lion is only a pair of jaws upon four legs. The kind of food determines the shape of tooth, jaw, shoulder-blade, muscle, and claw, and explains the majesty. And in exactly the same manner, that which under certain circumstances seems a foul, despicable crime, reveals itself, regarded from another standpoint, to be a miniature edition of one of the grand, brilliant vices of which history tells—and this is Balzac's standpoint.

Even in as early a work as *Eugenie Grandet* we come upon expressions which prove it. The time is approaching when Eugenie will be forced to confess to the miser who is her father that she no longer possesses her ducats, that she has actually given them away. "Three days later," writes Balzac, "a terrible drama was to be enacted—a bourgeois tragedy without poison, dagger, or bloodshed, yet more cruel than any of those which happened in the famous family of the Atrides." This is as much as to say: My middle-class novel is more tragic than your classic tragedy. In *Pere Goriot*, when the mistress of the famous boarding-house is loudly and despairingly bewailing the departure of her boarders, Balzac remarks: "the lamentations which Lord Byron has put into the mouth of Tasso are beautiful, but they lack the profound truth of Madame Vauquer's." Which means: The pettiness and vulgarity which I describe is, vigorously apprehended, more interesting than all your noble generalities. In *Cesar Birotteau* Balzac not only makes jesting reference in his titles to Montesquieu's famous book on the Roman Empire, but, with the audacity of genius, compares his elaborate, lengthy description of a clever Parisian perfumer's successes and misfortunes with the story of the Trojan wars and the changeful fortunes of Napoleon. "Troy and Napoleon are only heroic epics. May this tale be an epic of middle-class life, of destinies to which no poet has turned his attention, so destitute of all greatness do they appear. Its subject is not a single man, but a whole host of sufferings." Which is as much as to say: In literature nothing is in itself little or great; in a poor hairdresser's struggle for existence I can read a heroic poem; I show how the events of a humble private life, if we connect them with their causes and trace these back to their source, are as important, as interesting and engrossing as the great revolutions in the lives of nations. And when, in that masterpiece, *Un Ménage de Garçon*, the cunning, handsome Max Gilet, is killed in a duel, the author observes: "Thus died one of those men who are capable of great things when their environment is favorable; a man whom nature had treated like a spoiled child, for she had given him the courage, the coolness, and the political sagacity of a Caesar Borgia." So effective is the last of these reflections, that the reader feels as if he had not understood Max's character until now, when he sees it in the light of this name.

And virtue is in Balzac's eyes just as much of a result as vice. Although he is at times weakly sentimental and bombastic in his descriptions of dutifulness and benevolence, to which he moreover imparts a strong Roman Catholic coloring, he never fails to direct attention to the sources of the virtues he describes, which are to be found, now in a natural frigidity of the senses, now in pride, now in unconscious calculation, now in inherited nobility of sentiment, now in feminine remorse, masculine simple-mindedness, or the pious hope of reward in a future life.

Un Ménage de Garçon, *Cousine Bette*, and *Les Illusions perdues* are works which ought to be read by any one who is desirous of appreciating the growth of their author's literary powers during the last stage of his career.

The first, which is one of Balzac's least known and read novels, is an admirable psychological analysis of the life of a small country-town and of a family with branches there and in Paris. The chief character is a decayed officer of Napoleon's Guards, originally a strong, energetic character, now the personification of brutal, passionate egoism. The second novel mentioned, *La Cousine Bette*, a well-known and much read one, gives an incomparable realistic representation of the ruinous power of the erotic passion. Even Shakespeare (in Antony and Cleopatra) does not treat the theme in a more masterly and convincing manner. *Les Illusions perdues* is devoted to demonstrating the degrading results of the abuse of the press.

The title of this last novel is characteristic of Balzac. It might, in a manner, be the title of his complete works. But no other single book of his gives such a good general idea of his attitude to modern civilization. The pernicious side of the influence of the newspaper press is treated as the dark side of public life generally.

Like most great authors who have not lived to be old, Balzac had little reason to rejoice over the criticism meted out to him by the press. He was not understood. Even the best critics, like Sainte-Beuve, were too unlike him and too near to him in time to understand his greatness. He lived a solitary life; contrary to Parisian custom he took no steps to get his books praised; and, as usually happens, such success as he earned procured him as much envy as fame. In *Les Illusions perdues* he gave a picture of the press for which the insulted journalists never forgave him. The most eminent of them was Jules Janin. His portrait was, not exactly ill-naturedly, but far from flatteringly painted in the novel under the name of Etienne Lousteau. This made and still makes his criticism of the book very amusing. It appeared in the *Revue de Paris*, a periodical to which Balzac had been a regular contributor until he brought and gained a lawsuit against it, after which it naturally treated him as an outlaw. It is a malicious, trivial, witty piece of writing, which has not survived the book it was intended to ruin.

A young, poor provincial poet, beautiful as a god, but of weak character and mediocre talent, is brought to Paris by the Muse of the Department, an elegant, aristocratic woman. They are in love with each other, and it has been the lady's intention to allow him to play the part of her accepted lover in the capital; but when she is received with open arms by the fashionable world, she suddenly sees herself and her knight in a new light. Coldness and neglect on her part ensue; Lucien is thrown into the shade by a more than middle-aged man of the world. And now we are called on to observe the stages of another of the many processes by which provincials are educated into Parisians. Lucien hopes to make his way as an author; he has written a novel in Sir Walter Scott's style and a volume of poems; he is received into a little circle of poor, proud young authors, artists, and scientific men, chosen spirits, to whom the future of France belongs. But the months of poverty, self-denial, laborious study, and ideal hope are too long for him; he pines for immediate pleasure and fame, for revenge upon all who humiliated him when he was the ignorant country prophet. The so-called "minor press" offers him the chance of completely satisfying his desire; his head is turned, and he plunges, without cause to advocate or principle to uphold, into daily journalism.

Lousteau takes him to the shop of a rich Palais-Royal bookseller and newspaper proprietor:

Each time the bookseller opened his lips he grew in Lucien's eyes; the young man seemed to see politics and literature converging towards this shop as their true centre. To find an eminent poet prostituting his muse to a journalist was a terrible lesson to the great man from the country. Money! In that word lies the solution of every problem. He is lonely, unknown, has only a doubtful friendship to look to for happiness. He blames his true and sorrowing friends of the literary brotherhood for having painted the world to him in false colours and having hindered him from rushing, pen in hand, into the great melee.

From the bookshop Lousteau and Lucien make their way to the theatre. Lousteau, as a journalist, is welcome everywhere. The manager tells them how a conspiracy against the play has been defeated by means of a free use of the purses of his two prettiest actresses' wealthy admirers.

During these last two hours Lucien had heard of nothing but money. Everything had resolved itself into money. At the theatre and in the bookshop, with publisher and with editor, there had been no question of art or real merit. He felt as if the huge stamping-machine of the mint were imprinting its mark with dull, heavy blows on his head and heart.

His literary conscience evaporates, and he becomes the literary and dramatic critic of an impudent, stupid newspaper. Loved and supported by an actress, he sinks ever deeper in the life led by the man who has sold his pen. He goes over from the Liberals to the Conservatives. The depth of his degradation is most strongly borne in upon us in the scene where, having been compelled by his editor to write a malicious attack on an admirable book written by the best and noblest of his own friends (Balzac's ideal author), he is found knocking at this friend's door, on the evening before the article appears, to beg his forgiveness. Outward is soon added to inward misery. His mistress dies, and he is in such straits that he has to write obscene songs sitting by her death-bed, to raise the money for her funeral expenses. He ends by accepting from her maid some money which the woman has just earned in a shameful manner, and with it paying for his journey home to his native village. And all this bears the stamp of truth—horrible truth. In this one book Balzac renounces the impartiality of the scientific observer. Everywhere else he preserves his equanimity; here he chastises with scorpions.

On William Dean Howells

Mark Twain

This essay is as valuable for what it reveals about the sensibilities of Mark Twain as it is for its discussion of William Dean Howells. As he praises Howells for his precise diction and subtle humor, we see that Mark Twain himself places a great deal of importance on the selection of the "right word," the execution of a humor that is "pervasive" but "makes no more show and no more noise than does the circulation of blood," and the avoidance of obvious devices and literary clichés. For more on Howells and Twain, see Howells' essay "Some Anomalies of the Short Story," and Brander Matthews' essay on Twain, also in this volume.

Is it true that the sun of a man's mentality touches noon at forty and then begins to wane toward setting? Doctor Osler is charged with saying so. Maybe he said it, maybe he didn't; I don't know which it is. But if he said it, I can point him to a case which proves his rule. Proves it by being an exception to it. To this place I nominate William Dean Howells.

I read his *Venetian Days* about forty years ago. I compare it with his paper on Machiavelli in a late number of *Harper*, and I cannot find that his English has suffered any impairment. For forty years his English has been to me a continual delight and astonishment. In the sustained exhibition of certain great qualities—clearness, compression, verbal exactness, and unforced and seemingly unconscious felicity of phrasing—he is, in my belief, without his peer in the English-writing world. Sustained. I entrench myself behind that protecting word. There are others who exhibit those great qualities as greatly as he does, but only by intervaled distributions of rich moonlight, with stretches of veiled and dimmer landscape between; whereas Howells' moon sails cloudless skies all night and all the nights.

In the matter of verbal exactness, Howells has no superior, I suppose. He seems to be almost always able to find that elusive and shifty grain of gold, the right word. Others have to put up with approximations, more or less frequently; he has better luck. To me, the others are miners working with the gold pan—of necessity some of the gold washes over and escapes; whereas, in my fancy, he is quicksilver riding down a riffle—no grain of the metal stands much chance of eluding him. A powerful agent is the right word: it lights the reader's way and makes it plain; a close approximation to it will answer, and much traveling is done in a well-enough fashion by its help, but we do not welcome it and applaud it and rejoice in it as we do when the right one blazes out on us. Whenever we come upon one of those intensely right words in a book or a newspaper the resulting effect is physical as well as spiritual, and electrically prompt: it tingles exquisitely around through the walls of the mouth and tastes as tart and crisp and good as the autumn-butter that creams the sumac-berry. One has no time to examine the word and vote upon its rank and standing, the automatic recognition of its supremacy is so immediate. There is a plenty of acceptable literature which deals largely in approximations, but it may be likened to a fine landscape seen through the rain; the right word would dismiss the rain, then you would see it better. It doesn't rain when Howells is at work.

And where does he get the easy and effortless flow of his speech, and its cadenced and undulating rhythm, and its architectural felicities of construction, its graces of expression, its pemmican quality of compression, and all that? Born to him, no doubt. All in shining good order in the beginning, all extraordinary; and all just as shining, just as extraordinary today, after forty years of diligent wear and tear and use. He passed his fortieth year long and long ago; but I think his English of today—his perfect English, I wish to say—can throw down the glove before his English of that antique time and not be afraid.

I will go back to the paper on Machiavelli now, and ask the reader to examine this passage from it which I append. I do not mean examine it in a bird's-eye way; I mean search it, study it. And, of course, read it aloud. I may be wrong, still it is my conviction that one cannot get out of finely wrought literature all that is in it by reading it mutely:

> Mr. Dyer is rather of the opinion, first luminously suggested by Macaulay, that Machiavelli was in earnest, but must not be judged as a political moralist of our time and race would be judged. He thinks that Machiavelli was in earnest, as none but an idealist can be, and he is the first to imagine him an idealist immersed in realities, who involuntarily transmutes the events under his eye into something like the visionary issues of reverie. The Machiavelli whom he depicts does not cease to be politically a republican and socially a just man because he holds up an atrocious despot like Caesar Borgia as a mirror for rulers. What Machiavelli beheld round him in Italy was a civic disorder in which there was oppression without statecraft, and revolt without patriotism. When a miscreant like Borgia appeared upon the scene and reduced both tyrants and rebels to an apparent quiescence, he might very well seem to such a dreamer the savior of society whom a certain sort of dreamers are always looking for. Machiavelli was no less honest when he honored the diabolical force of Caesar Borgia than Carlyle was when at different times he extolled the strong man who destroys liberty in creating order. But Carlyle has only just ceased to be mistaken for a reformer, while it is still Machiavelli's hard fate to be

so trammeled in his material that his name stands for whatever is most malevolent and perfidious in human nature.

You see how easy and flowing it is; how unvexed by ruggednesses, clumsinesses, broken meters, how simple and—so far as you or I can make out—unstudied; how clear, how limpid, how understandable, how unconfused by cross-currents, eddies, undertows; how seemingly unadorned, yet is all adornment, like the lily-of-the-valley; and how compressed, how compact, without a complacency-signal hung out anywhere to call attention to it.

There are twenty-three lines in the quoted passage. After reading it several times aloud, one perceives that a good deal of matter is crowded into a small space. I think it is a model of compactness. When I take its materials apart and work them over and put them together in my way, I find I cannot crowd the result back into the same hole, there not being room enough.

The proffered paragraph is a just and fair sample; the rest of the article is as compact as it is; there are no waste words. The sample is just in other ways: limpid, fluent, graceful, and rhythmical as it is, it holds no superiority in these respects over the rest of the essay. Also, the choice of phrasing noticeable in the sample is not lonely; there is a plenty of its kin distributed through the other paragraphs. This is claiming much when that kin must face the challenge of a phrase like the one in the middle sentence: "an idealist immersed in realities who involuntarily transmutes the events under his eye into something like the visionary issues of reverie." With a hundred words to do it with, the literary artisan could catch that airy thought and tie it down and reduce it to a concrete condition, visible, substantial, understandable and all right, like a cabbage; but the artist does it with twenty, and the result is a flower.

The quoted phrase, like a thousand others that have come from the same source, has the quality of certain scraps of verse which take hold of us and stay in our memories. We do not understand why, at first: all the words being the right words, none of them is conspicuous, and so they all seem inconspicuous, therefore we wonder what it is about them that makes their message take hold.

> The mossy marbles rest
> On the lips that he has prest
> In their bloom,
> And the names he loved to hear
> Have been carved for many a year
> On the tomb.

It is like a dreamy strain of moving music, with no sharp notes in it. The words are all "right" words, and all the same size. We do not notice it at first. We get the effect, it goes straight home to us, but we do not know why. It is when the right words are conspicuous that they thunder:

> The glory that was Greece and the grandeur that was Rome!

When I go back from Howells old to Howells young I find him arranging and clustering English words well, but not any better than now. He is not more felicitous in concreting abstractions now than he was in translating, then, the visions of the eyes of flesh into words that reproduced their forms and colors:

> In Venetian streets they give the fallen snow no rest. It is at once shoveled into the canals by hundreds of half-naked *facchini,* and now in St. Mark's Place the music of innumerable shovels smote upon my ear; and I saw the shivering legion of poverty as it engaged the elements in a struggle for the possession of the Piazza. But the snow continued to fall, and through the twilight of the descending flakes all this toil and encounter looked like that weary kind of effort in

dreams, when the most determined industry seems only to renew the task. The lofty crest of the bell-tower was hidden in the folds of falling snow, and I could no longer see the golden angel upon its summit. But looked at across the Piazza, the beautiful outline of St. Mark's Church was perfectly penciled in the air, and the shifting threads of the snowfall were woven into a spell of novel enchantment around the structure that always seemed to me too exquisite in its fantastic loveliness to be anything but the creation of magic. The tender snow had compassionated the beautiful edifice for all the wrongs of time, and so hid the stains and ugliness of decay that it looked as if just from the hand of the builder—or, better said, just from the brain of the architect. There was marvelous freshness in the colors of the mosaics in the great arches of the facade, and all that gracious harmony into which the temple rises, of marble scrolls and leafy exuberance airily supporting the statues of the saints, was a hundred times etherealized by the purity and whiteness of the drifting flakes. The snow lay lightly on the golden globes that tremble like peacock-crests above the vast domes, and plumed them with softest white; it robed the saints in ermine; and it danced over all its work, as if exulting in its beauty—beauty which filled me with subtle, selfish yearning to keep such evanescent loveliness for the little-while-longer of my whole life, and with despair, to think that even the poor lifeless shadow of it could never be fairly reflected in picture or poem.

Through the wavering snowfall, the Saint Theodore upon one of the granite pillars of the Piazzetta did not show so grim as his wont is, and the winged lion on the other might have been a winged lamb, so gentle and mild he looked by the tender light of the storm. The towers of the island churches loomed faint and far away in the dimness; the sailors in the rigging of the ships that lay in the Basin wrought like phantoms among the shrouds; the gondolas stole in and out of the opaque distance more noiselessly and dreamily than ever; and a silence, almost palpable, lay upon the mutest city in the world.

The spirit of Venice is there: of a city where Age and Decay, weary from distributing damage and repulsiveness among the other cities of the planet in accordance with the policy and business of their profession, come for rest and play between seasons, and treat themselves to the luxury and relaxation of sinking the shop and inventing and squandering charms all about, instead of abolishing such as they find, as is their habit when not on vacation.

In the working season they do business in Boston sometimes, and a character in *The Undiscovered Country* takes accurate note of pathetic effects wrought by them upon the aspects of a street of once dignified and elegant homes whose occupants have moved away and left them a prey to neglect and gradual ruin and progressive degradation; a descent which reaches bottom at last, when the street becomes a roost for humble professionals of the faith-cure and fortune-telling sort:

> What a queer, melancholy house, what a queer, melancholy street! I don't think I was ever in a street before where quite so many professional ladies, with English surnames, preferred Madam to Mrs. on their door-plates. And the poor old place has such a desperately conscious air of going to the deuce. Every house seems to wince as you go by, and button itself up to the chin for fear you should find out it had no shirt on—so to speak. I don't know what's the reason, but these material tokens of a social decay afflict me terribly; a tipsy woman isn't dreadfuler than a haggard old house, that's once been a home, in a street like this.

Howells' pictures are not mere stiff, hard, accurate photographs; they are photographs with feeling in them, and sentiment, photographs taken in a dream, one might say.

As concerns his humor, I will not try to say anything, yet I would try, if I had the words that might approximately reach up to is high place. I do not think any one else can play with humorous fancies so gracefully and delicately and deliciously as he does, nor has so many to play with, nor can come so near making them look as if they were doing the playing themselves and he was not aware that they were at it. For they are unobtrusive, and quiet in their ways, and well conducted. His is a humor which flows softly all around about and over and through the mesh of the page, pervasive, refreshing, health-giving, and makes no more show and no more noise than does the circulation of the blood.

There is another thing which is contentingly noticeable in Howells' books. That is his "stage directions"—those artifices which authors employ to throw a kind of human naturalness around a scene and a conversation, and help the reader to see the one and get at meanings in the other which might not be perceived if entrusted unexplained to the bare words of talk. Some authors overdo the stage directions, they elaborate them quite beyond necessity; they spend so much time and take up so much room in telling us how a person said a thing and how he looked and acted when he said it that we get tired and vexed and wish he hadn't said it at all. Other authors' directions are brief enough, but it is seldom that the brevity contains either wit or information. Writers of this school go in rags, in the matter of stage directions; the majority of them have nothing in stock but a cigar, a laugh, a blush, and a bursting into tears. In their poverty they work these sorry things to the bone. They say:

". . . replied Alfred, flipping the ash from his cigar." (This explains nothing; it only wastes space.)

". . . responded Richard, with a laugh." (There was nothing to laugh about; there never is. The writer puts it in from habit—automatically; he is paying no attention to his work, or he would see that there is nothing to laugh at; often, when a remark is unusually and poignantly flat and silly, he tries to deceive the reader by enlarging the stage direction and making Richard break into "frenzies of uncontrollable laughter." This makes the reader sad.)

". . . murmured Gladys, blushing." (This poor old shopworn blush is a tiresome thing. We get so we would rather Gladys would fall out of the book and break her neck than do it again. She is always doing it, and usually irrelevantly. Whenever it is her turn to murmur she hangs out her blush; it is the only thing she's got. In a little while we hate her, just as we do Richard.)

". . . repeated Evelyn, bursting into tears." (This kind keeps a book damp all the time. They can't say a thing without crying. They cry so much about nothing that by and by when they have something to cry about they have gone dry; they sob, and fetch nothing; we are not moved. We are only glad.)

They gravel me, these stale and overworked stage directions, these carbon films that got burnt out long ago and cannot now carry any faintest thread of light. It would be well if they could be relieved of duty and flung out in the literary back yard to rot and disappear along with the discarded and forgotten "steeds" and "halidomes" and similar stage-properties once so dear to our grandfathers. But I am friendly to Howells' stage directions; more friendly to them than to anyone else's, I think. They are done with a competent and discriminating art, and are faithful to the requirements of a stage direction's proper and lawful office, which is to inform. Sometimes they convey a scene and its conditions so well that I believe I could see the scene and get the spirit and meaning of the accompanying dialogue if some one would read merely the stage directions to me and leave out the talk. For instance, a scene like this, from *The Undiscovered Country*:

". . . and she laid her arms with a beseeching gesture on her father's shoulder."

". . . she answered, following his gesture with a glance."

". . . she said, laughing nervously."

"... she asked, turning swiftly upon him that strange, searching glance."

"... she answered, vaguely."

"... she reluctantly admitted."

"... but her voice died wearily away, and she stood looking into his face with puzzled entreaty."

Howells does not repeat his forms, and does not need to; he can invent fresh ones without limit. It is mainly the repetition over and over again, by the third-rates, of worn and commonplace and juiceless forms that makes their novels such a weariness and vexation to us, I think. We do not mind one or two deliveries of their wares, but as we turn the pages over and keep on meeting them we presently get tired of them and wish they would do other things for a change:

"... replied Alfred, flipping the ash from his cigar."

"... responded Richard, with a laugh."

"... repeated Evelyn, bursting into tears."

"... replied the Earl, flipping the ash from his cigar."

"... responded the undertaker, with a laugh."

"... murmured the chambermaid, blushing."

"... replied the conductor, flipping the ash from his cigar."

"... responded Arkwright, with a laugh."

"... murmured the chief of police, blushing."

"... repeated the house-cat, bursting into tears."

And so on and so on; till at last it ceases to excite. I always notice stage directions, because they fret me and keep me trying to get out of their way, just as the automobiles do. At first; then by and by they become monotonous and I get run over.

Howells has done much work, and the spirit of it is as beautiful as the make of it. I have held him in admiration and affection for so many years that I know by the number of those years that he is old now; but his heart isn't, nor is his pen—and years do not count. Let him have plenty of them: there is profit in them for us.

Some Anomalies of the Short Story

William Dean Howells

Howells, an important figure in the realistic fiction of early 20th-century American literature, sets forth in this essay his ideas on issues that remain of concern to academics, writers, and editors as the century approaches its end. One such issue: Why did collections of short stories perform so poorly in the marketplace, while individual stories appearing in literary journals and magazines were quite successful? This is a condition that has persisted to the present day. Does the fault lie with publishers, with the writers, with the short story as a form, or with the reading public itself? Howells offers, if not concrete answers, engaging illuminations of the questions. Beyond these issues, Howells also presents his thoughts on the relationship between the short story and other narrative forms, its prospects for historical endurance, and the international nature of its formal development.

The interesting experiment of one of our great publishing houses in putting out serially several volumes of short stories, with the hope that a courageous persistence may overcome the popular indifference to such collections when severally administered, suggest some questions as to this eldest form of fiction which I should like to ask the reader's patience with. I do not know that I shall be able to answer them, or that I shall try to do so; the vitality of a question that is answered seems to exhale in the event; it palpitates no longer; curiosity flutters away from the faded flower, which is fit then only to be folded away in the *hortus siccus* of accomplished facts. In view of this I may wish merely to state the problems and leave them for the reader's solution, or, more amusingly, for his mystification.

I

One of the most amusing questions concerning the short story is why a form which is singly so attractive that every one likes to read a short story when he finds it alone is collectively so repellent as it is said to be. Before now I have imagined the case to be somewhat the same as that of a number of pleasant people who are most acceptable as separate householders, but who lose caste and cease to be desirable acquaintances when gathered into a boarding-house.

Yet the case is not the same quite, for we see that the short story where it is ranged with others of its species within the covers of a magazine is so welcome that the editor thinks his issue the more brilliant the more short story writers he can call about his board, or under the roof of his *pension*. Here the boarding-house analogy breaks, breaks so signally that I was lately moved to ask a distinguished editor why a book of short stories usually failed and a magazine usually succeeded because of them. He answered, gayly, that the short stories in most books of them were bad; that where they were good, they went; and he alleged several well-known instances in which books of prime short stories had a great vogue. He was so handsomely interested in my inquiry that I could not well say I thought some of the short stories which he had boasted in his last issue were mediocre, and yet, as he allowed, had mainly helped sell it. I had in mind many books of short stories of the first excellence which had failed as decidedly as those others had succeeded, for no reason that I could see; possibly there is really no reason in any literary success or failure that can be predicted, or applied in another case.

I could name these books, if it would serve any purpose, but in my doubt, I will leave the reader to think of them, for I believe that his indolence or intellectual reluctance is largely to blame for the failure of good books of short stories. He is commonly so averse to any imaginative exertion that he finds it a hardship to respond to that peculiar demand which a book of good short stories makes upon him. He can read one good short story in a magazine with refreshment, and a pleasant sense of excitement, in the sort of spur it gives to his own constructive faculty. But, if this is repeated in ten or twenty stories, he becomes fluttered and exhausted by the draft upon his energies; whereas a continuous fiction of the same quantity acts as an agreeable sedative. A condition that the short story tacitly makes with the reader, through its limitations, is that he shall subjectively fill in the details and carry out the scheme which in its small dimensions the story can only suggest; and the greater number of readers find this too much for their feeble powers, while they cannot resist the incitement to attempt it.

My theory does not wholly account for the fact (no theory wholly accounts for any fact), and I own that the same objections would lie from the reader against a number of short stories in a magazine. But it may be that the effect is not the same in the magazine because of the variety in the authorship, and because it would be impossibly jolting to read all the short stories in a magazine *seriatim*. On the other hand, the identity of authorship gives a continuity of attraction to the short stories in a book which forms that exhausting strain upon the imagination of the involuntary copartner.

II

Then, what is the solution as to the form of publication for short stories, since people do not object to them singly but collectively, and not in variety, but in identity of authorship? Are they to be printed only in the magazines, or are they to be collected in volumes combining a variety of authorship? Rather, I could wish, it might be found feasible to purvey them in some pretty shape where each would appeal singly to the reader and would not exhaust him in the subjective after-work required of him. In this event many short stories now cramped into undue limits by the editorial exigencies of the magazines might expand to greater length and breadth, and without ceasing to be each a short story might not make so heavy a demand upon the subliminal forces of the reader.

If any one were to say that all this was a little fantastic, I should not contradict him; but I hope there is some reason in it, if reason can help the short story to greater favor, for it is a form which I have great pleasure in as a reader, and pride in as an American. If we have not excelled all other moderns in it, we have certainly excelled in it; possibly because we are in the period of our literary development which corresponds to that of other peoples when the short story pre-eminently flourished among them. But when one has said a thing like this, it immediately accuses one of loose and inaccurate statement, and requires one to refine upon it, either for one's own peace of conscience or for one's safety from the thoughtful reader. I am not much afraid of that sort of reader, for he is very rare, but I do like to know myself what I mean, if I mean anything in particular.

In this instance I am obliged to ask myself whether our literary development can be recognized separately from that of the whole English-speaking world. I think it can, though, as I am always saying American literature is merely a condition of English literature. For in some sense every European literature is a condition of some other European literature, yet the impulse in each eventuates, if it does not originate indigenously. A younger literature will choose, by a sort of natural selection, some things for assimilation from an elder literature, for no more apparent reason than it will reject other things, and it will transform them in the process so that it will give them the effect of indigeneity. The short story among the Italians, who called it the novella, and supplied us with the name devoted solely among us to fiction of epical magnitude, refined indefinitely upon the Greek romance, if it derived from that; it retrenched itself in scope, and enlarged itself in the variety of its types. But still these remained types, and they remained types with the French imitators of the Italian novella. It was not till the Spanish borrowed the form of the novella that it began to bear character, and to fruit in the richness of picaresque fiction. When the English borrowed it they adapted it, in the metrical tales of Chaucer, to the genius of their nation, which was then both poetical and humorous. Here it was full of character, too, and more and more personality began to enlarge the bounds of the conventional types and to imbue fresh ones. But in so far as the novella was studied in the Italian sources, the French, Spanish, and English literatures were conditions of Italian literature as distinctly, though, of course, not so thoroughly, as American literature is a condition of English literature. Each borrower gave a national cast to the thing borrowed, and that is what has happened with us, in the full measure that our nationality has differenced itself from the English.

Whatever truth there is in all this, and I will confess that a good deal of it seems to me hardy conjecture, rather favors my position that we are in some such period of our literary development as those other peoples when the short story flourished among them. Or, if I restrict our claim, I may safely claim that they abundantly had the novella when they had not the novel at all, and we now abundantly have the novella, while we have the novel only subordinately and of at least no such quantitative importance as the English, French, Spanish, Norwegians, Russians, and some others of our esteemed contemporaries, not to name the Italians. We surpass the Germans, who, like ourselves, have as distinctly excelled in the modern novella as they have fallen short in the novel. Or, if I may not quite say this, I will make bold to say that I can think of many German novelle that I should like to read again, but scarcely one German novel; and I could honestly say the same of American novelle, though not of American novels.

III

The abeyance, not to say the desuetude, that the novella fell into for several centuries is very curious, and fully as remarkable as the modern rise of the short story. It began to prevail in the dramatic form, for a play is a short story put on the stage; it may have satisfied in that form the early love of it, and it has continued to please in that form; but in its original shape it quite vanished, unless we consider the little studies and sketches and allegories of the *Spectator* and *Tattler* and *Idler* and *Rambler* and their imitations on the Continent as guises of the novella. The germ of the modern short story may have survived in these, or in the metrical form of the novella which appeared in Chaucer and never wholly disappeared. With Crabbe the novella became as distinctly the short story as it has become in the hands of Wilkins. But it was not till our time that its great merit as a form was felt, for until our time so great work was never done with it. I remind myself of Boccaccio, and of the *Arabian Nights*, without the wish to hedge from my bold stand. They are all elemental; compared with some finer modern work which deepens inward immeasurably, they are all of their superficial limits. They amuse, but they do not hold, the mind and stamp it with large and profound impressions.

I will own my suspicion that the perfection of the Italian work is philological rather than artistic, while the web woven by James or Jewett, by Kielland or Bjornson, by Maupassant, by Palacio Valdes, by Giovanni Verga, by Turgenev, in one of those little frames seems to me of an exquisite color and texture and of an entire literary preciousness, not only as regards the diction, but as regards those more intangible graces of form, those virtues of truth and reality, and those lasting significances which distinguish the masterpiece. The novella has in fact been carried so far in the short story that it might be asked whether it had not left the novel behind, as to perfection of form; though one might not like to affirm this. Yet there have been but few modern fictions of the novel's dimensions which have the beauty of form many a novella embodies. Is this because it is easier to give form in the small than in the large, or only because it is easier to hide formlessness? It is easier to give form in the novella than in the novel, because the design of less scope can be more definite, and because the persons and facts are fewer, and each can be more carefully treated. But, on the other hand, the slightest error in execution shows more in the small than in the large, and a fault of conception is more evident. The novella must be clearly imagined, above all things, for there is no room in it for those felicities of characterization or comment by which the artist of faltering design saves himself in the novel.

IV

The question as to where the short story distinguishes itself from the anecdote is of the same nature as that which concerns the boundary set between it and the novel. In both cases the difference of the novella is in the motive, or the origination. The anecdote is too palpably simple and single to be regarded as a novella, though there is now and then a novella like "The Father," by Bjornson, which is of the actual brevity of the anecdote, but which, when released in the reader's consciousness, expands to dramatic dimensions impossible to the anecdote. Many anecdotes have come down from antiquity, but not, I believe, one short story, at least in prose; and the Italians, if they did not invent the story, gave us something most sensibly distinguishable from the classic anecdote in the novella. The anecdote offers an illustration of character, or records a moment of action; the novella embodies a drama and develops a type.

It is not quite so clear as to when and where a piece of fiction ceases to be a novella and becomes a novel. The frontiers are so vague that one is obliged to recognize a middle species, or rather a middle magnitude, which paradoxically, but necessarily enough, we call the novelette. First we have the short story, or novella, then we have the long story, or novel, and between these we have the novelette, which is in name smaller than the short story, though it is in point of fact two or three times longer than a short story. We may realize them physically if we will adopt the magazine parlance and speak of the novella as a one-number story, of the novel as a serial, and of the novelette as a two-number or three-number story; if it passes the three-number limit it seems to become a novel. As a two-number or three-number story it is the despair of editors and publishers. The interest of so brief a serial will not mount sufficiently to carry strongly over from month to month; when the tale is completed it will not make a book which the industry (inexorable force!) cares to handle. It is therefore still awaiting its authoritative avatar, which it will be someone's prosperity and glory to imagine; for in the novelette are possibilities for fiction as yet scarcely divined.

The novelette can have almost as perfect form as the novella. In fact, the novel has form in the measure that it approaches the novelette; and some of the most symmetrical modern novels are scarcely more than novelettes, like Turgenev's *Dmitri Rudine*, or his *Smoke*, or *Spring Floods*. *The Vicar of Wakefield*, the father of the modern novel, is scarcely more than a novelette, and I have sometimes fancied, but no doubt vainly, that the ultimate novel might be of the dimensions of *Hamlet*. If any one should say there was not room in *Hamlet* for the character and incident requisite in a novel, I should be ready to answer that there seemed a good deal of both in *Hamlet*.

But no doubt there are other reasons why the novel should not finally be of the length of *Hamlet*, and I must not let my enthusiasm for the novelette carry me too far, or, rather, bring me up too short. I am disposed to dwell upon it, I suppose, because it has not yet shared the favor which the novella and the novel have enjoyed, and because until somebody invents a path for it to the public it cannot prosper like the one-number story or the serial. I should like to say as my last word for it here that I believe there are many novels which, if stripped of their padding, would turn out to have been all along merely novelettes in disguise.

It does not follow, however, that there are many novelle which, if they were duly padded, would be found novelettes. In that dim, subjective region where the aesthetic origins present themselves almost with the authority of inspirations there is nothing clearer than the difference between the short-story motive and the long-story motive. One, if one is in that line of work, feels instinctively just the size and carrying power of the given motive. Or, if the reader prefers a different figure, the mind which the seed has been dropped into from somewhere is mystically aware whether the seed is going to grow up a bush or is going to grow up a tree, if left to itself. Of course, the mind to which the seed is intrusted may play it false, and wilfully dwarf the growth, or force it to unnatural dimensions; but the critical observer will easily detect the fact of such treasons. Almost in the first germinal impulse the inventive mind forefeels the ultimate difference and recognizes the essential simplicity or complexity of the motive. There will be a prophetic subdivision into a variety of motives and a multiplication of characters and incidents and situations; or the original motive will be divined indivisible, and there will be a small group of people immediately interested and controlled by a single, or predominant, fact. The uninspired may contend that this is bosh, and I own that something might be said for their contention, but upon the whole I think it is gospel.

The right novel is never a grouping of novelle, as it might appear to the uninspired. If it indulges even in episodes, it loses in reality and vitality. It is one stock from which its various branches put out, and form it a living growth identical throughout. The right novella is never a novel cropped back from the size of a tree to a bush, or the branch of a tree stuck into the ground and made to serve for a bush. It is another species, destined by the agencies at work in the realm of unconsciousness to be brought into being of its own kind, and not of another.

V

This was always its case, but in the process of time the short story, while keeping the natural limits of the primal novella (if ever there was one), has shown almost limitless possibilities within them. It has shown itself capable of imparting the effect of every sort of intention, whether of humor or pathos, of tragedy or comedy or broad farce or delicate irony, of character or action. The thing that first made itself known as a little tale, usually salacious, dealing with conventionalized types and conventionalized incidents, has proved itself possibly the most flexible of all the literary forms in its adaptation to the needs of the mind that wishes to utter itself, inventively or constructively, upon some fresh occasion, or wishes briefly to criticise or represent some phase or fact of life.

The riches in this shape of fiction are effectively inestimable, if we consider what has been done in the short story, and is still doing everywhere. The good novels may be easily counted, but the good novelle, since Boccaccio began (if it was he that first began) to make them, cannot be computed. In quantity they are inexhaustible, and in quality they are wonderfully satisfying. Then why is it that so very, very few of the most satisfactory of that innumerable multitude stay by you, as people say, in characterization of action? How hard it is to recall a person or a fact out of any of them, out of the most signally good! We seem to be delightfully nourished as we read, but is it, after all, a full meal? We become of a perfect intimacy and a devoted friendship with the men and women in the short stories, but not apparently of a lasting acquaintance. It is a single meeting we have with them, and though we instantly love or hate them dearly, recurrence and repetition seem necessary to that familiar knowledge in which we hold the personages in a novel.

It is here that the novella, so much more perfect in form, shows its irremediable inferiority to the novel, and somehow to the play, to the very farce, which it may quantitatively excel. We can all recall by name many characters out of comedies and farces; but how many characters out of short stories can we recall? Most persons of the drama give themselves away by name for types, mere figments of allegory, and perhaps oblivion is the penalty that the novella pays for the fineness of its characterizations; but perhaps, also, the dramatic form has greater facilities for repetition, and so can stamp its persons more indelibly on the imagination than the narrative form in the same small space. The narrative must give to description what the drama trusts to representation; but this cannot account for the superior permanency of the dramatic types in so great measure as we might at first imagine, for they remain as much in mind from reading as from seeing the plays. It is possible that as the novella becomes more conscious, its persons will become more memorable; but as it is, though we now vividly and with lasting delight remember certain short stories, we scarcely remember by name any of the people in them. I may be risking too much in offering an instance, but who, in even such signal instances as "The Revolt of Mother," by Wilkins, or "The Dulham Ladies," by Jewett, can recall by name the characters that made them delightful?

VI

The defect of the novella which we have been acknowledging seems an essential limitation; but perhaps it is not insuperable; and we may yet have short stories which shall supply the delighted imagination with creations of as much immortality as we can reasonably demand. The structural change would not be greater than the moral or material change which has been wrought in it since it began as a yarn, gross and palpable, which the narrator spun out of the coarsest and often the filthiest stuff, to snare the thick fancy or amuse the lewd leisure of listeners willing as children to hear the same persons and the same things over and over again. Now it has not only varied the persons and things, but it has refined and verified them in the direction of the natural and the supernatural, until it is above all other literary forms the vehicle of reality and spirituality. When one thinks of a bit of James' psychology in this form, or a bit of Verga's or Kielland's sociology, or a bit of Jewett's exquisite veracity, one perceives the immense distance which the short story has come on the way to the height it has reached. It serves equally the ideal and the real; that which it is loath to serve is the unreal, so that among the short stories which have recently made reputations for their authors very few are of that peculiar cast which we have no name for but Romantic. The only distinguished modern writer of Romantic novelle whom I can think of is Bret Harte, and he is of a period when Romanticism was so imperative as to be almost a condition of fiction. I am never so enamored of a cause that I will not admit facts that seem to tell against it, and I will allow that this writer of Romantic short stories has more than any other supplied us with memorable types and characters. We remember John Oakhurst by name; we remember Kentuck and Tennessee's Partner, at least by nickname; and we remember their several qualities. These figures, if we cannot quite consent that they are persons, exist in our memories by force of their creator's imagination, and at the moment I cannot think of any others that do, out of the myriad of American short stories, except Rip Van Winkle out of Irving's "Legend of Sleepy Hollow," and Marjorie Daw out of Aldrich's famous little caprice of that title, and James's Daisy Miller.

It appears to be the fact that those writers who have first distinguished themselves in the novella have seldom written novels of prime order. Kipling is an eminent example, but he has yet a long life before him in which to upset any theory about him, and one can only instance him provisionally. On the other hand, one can be much more confident that the best novelle have been written by the greatest novelists, conspicuously Maupassant, Verga, Bjornson, Thomas Hardy, James, Cable, Turgenev, Tolstoy, Valdes, not to name others. These have, in fact, all done work so good in this form that one is tempted to call it their best work. It is really not their best, but it is work so good that it ought to have equal acceptance with their novels, if that distinguished editor was right who said that short stories sold well when they were good short stories. That they ought to do so is so evident that a devoted reader of them, to whom I was submitting the anomaly the other day, insisted that they did. I could only allege the testimony of publishers and authors to the contrary, and this did not satisfy him.

It does not satisfy me, and I wish that the general reader, with whom the fault lies, could be made to say why, if he likes one short story by itself and four short stories in a magazine, he does not like, or will not have, a dozen short stories in a book. This was the baffling question which I began with and which I find myself forced to end with, after all the light I have thrown upon the subject. I leave it where I found it, but perhaps that is a good deal for a critic to do. If I had left it anywhere else the reader might not feel bound to deal with it practically by reading all the books of short stories he could lay hands on, and either divining why he did not enjoy them, or else forever foregoing his prejudice *against* them because of his pleasure *in* them.

A cumulative index to all authors and stories in the complete 10 volume set of **The World's Best Short Stories** is included in Volume IX.